Income Innovations

Income Innovations

How New Markets Are Improving The Way People Make Money… And How You Can Too!

Harvey Hess

On the Inside Press
Beverly Hills, CA

Income Innovations: How New Markets are Improving the Way People Make Money…And How You Can Too!

www.EverydaysASaturday.com
Harvey@HarveyHess.com

Published by On the Inside Press
Beverly Hills, CA 90210
www.OntheInsidePress.com

Library of Congress Control Number 2015901722
ISBN 978-1-942707-03-5

Cover design by David T. Fagan and Carli Smith.

Printed in the United State of America.

First Printing

Table of Contents

Foreword

What does it take to follow your dreams, goals, and ambitions – and live a life you are truly passionate about? That's a question that has resonated with me since I was a young kid while growing up in the ghettos of Northern California. As I was surrounded with struggle, lack, and limitation, the thought would keep popping up in my mind – why are some living their dreams while others aren't?

Fortunately, the old adage has validity to it: ask and you shall receive. I kept asking that question, and little by little answers would come to me. Answers in the form of a book, an audio, a seminar, or a mentor. These answers eventually led me to being able to generate a multi-seven figure income and live the life of my dreams – all before turning thirty.

However, it's important to note that none of this was by accident. All of my fortunes, in leaving a legacy for others and in wealth, have all happened on purpose, and with purpose. That is really what life is all about. It is not about drudging to a job you do not really like, or making just enough money to make ends meet. For many, however, that seems to be their current lot in life. But it really is a choice. You have a choice, you have a voice, you have a purpose.

My life could have been so different if I had just accepted what others around me thought of as a lack of opportunity. I was born in poverty, in Mississippi. After graduating from the crib, my bed became a blanket underneath the crib. Looking for a better life, my mother moved us to an industrial city in California called Pittsburg. We were still in the ghetto. I use to go to sleep at night hearing gunshots in the neighborhood. I could have conformed. I could have just said, "That's all there is, that's all."

Thankfully, I wanted more out of life, knew there was more in life, knew I could be someone. And since you are reading this book – I know you want more as well.

Today, as I look over what has transpired for the past few decades, I am happy, I am grateful, I am hopefully leaving a legacy for others to follow. I speak to thousands every year and have been to over 35 countries on speaking engagements, speaking to people – just like you – who are looking for more, who understand that they have a purpose here on this earth, that they control the outcome, and can do whatever it is they want to do.

Entrepreneurship is becoming a hot topic. The end of many blue collar and white collar jobs is forcing folks to reinvent. Change happens. The changes we are seeing this century, thus far, are the widest reaching in regards to jobs, job formation, and career advancement in our lifetime. People are having to look elsewhere, and starting your own business is where many are looking. It truly is becoming the rise of the entrepreneur.

That is how I met Harvey Hess. Somewhere around the turn of the century, 2000 or 2001, Harvey came to one of my public seminars in Phoenix, Arizona (I do many private Company events too). He came there looking to reinvent, looking to the next chapter of his life. My teachings always revolve around personal development, something we all should being doing all the time, but many do not. Harvey was all about learning, all about expanding his horizons on what was available outside of the status quo. In all, over the past 10 years, every time I was in the Phoenix area, Harvey was present, and so were those he was mentoring.

And now, he has written a book about this experience, about what to know, and what it takes to break out, to break away and do life on purpose, not by accident. It has some real, practical advice and instruction, as well as some education on this new connection economy which is developing.

No book or seminar can promise you that you will be a success by just following its advice, I wish there were one, but is not about the words written in a book. It is all about you, what actions you take based upon the advice, based upon the new information you take from the book. Knowledge is powerful, but finding your purpose and believing and acting upon your belief is what separates those who leave a legacy and those who wander around in mediocrity so as to arrive at their grave safely.

I hope you find your why, leave your legacy, and my wish is the information you are about to read will assist you in getting there.

Jerry "DRhino" Clark
Chief Empowerment Officer
ClubRhino.com

Preface

When I began to think about writing this book, it was at a time when I was searching for a way to help others navigate the new business world in which we are now living. The Industrial Revolution is dead. The old way of working for an employer, as we have known it, is dead. If you were born between 1946 and 1985, you may feel cheated: you most likely bought into the wrong system. The old system is dead, even though our schools and universities are still trying to churn out "employees." We were sold a bill of goods, the old "get a good education, find a good company to work for, show up every day and contribute, get the few weeks off a year, retire at 65 with a pension and the gold watch" life plan. That was the Industrial Economy. We all conformed. We were brought up in a world that encouraged complacency and encouraged conformity. Do not think; just do. Do not rock the boat, just do what you are told. Do not think out of the box, conform. Do not be stupid, be safe. Do what everyone else is doing, has always done.

It does not mean that the old Industrial Economy will go away; we will still need coal and oil to be extracted, still need worker bees in various industries. But for most of us, it is over. The race to the bottom—lower prices, more efficiencies, lower quality, even more efficiencies in the system, lower wages, production outside North America—is just about done, finished, kaput. No one really wins the race to the bottom, everyone loses, and we are now discovering that indeed. It is not the go forward model for the world however, and especially for the U.S. and Canada.

The most recent statistics on job satisfaction clearly state that 80 percent of those employed hate their jobs and are not satisfied with what they do for a living. If that is the case, then it is no surprise that various "happiness indexes" from around the world place the U.S.A. somewhere between sixth and tenth in overall happiness, despite being the most prosperous country in the world. A recent Mayo Clinic study found that 70 percent of the U.S. population is taking at least one prescription drug, with more than 50 percent talking two or more prescription drugs every day and 20 percent taking five or more! The worst part of the study is that 13 percent of drugs taken daily are antidepressants. This, again, in the most prosperous country in the world. These are really sick numbers (pun intended!), and I believe a contributing factor is that most people do not have a clue as to why they do what they do for a living; they don't know what purpose they have in our world or even in their own life. We are not trained to think for ourselves; we don't know how to find our *why*, our passion, our purpose and then do what makes us happy. We just learned how to conform, without a purpose. Simon Sinek, author of *Start With Why*, recently put it this way: "Most of us live our lives by accident—we live it as it happens. Fulfillment comes when we live our lives on purpose."

However, there is a revolution going on today, especially with the "Generation Y" members, those born between 1977 and 1995. They are starting to get it: to discover that we are moving into a Connection Economy and completely away from the 150-year-old Industrial Economy. But if you are a member of Generation X (1965–1976) or a Baby Boomer (1946–1964), or even a Traditionalist (pre-1946), you are probably scratching your head, wondering what is happening.

It is time to quit wondering, to get over it, to pull up the bootstraps, to find out what really makes your engine roar, and make to the second part of your life special, leave a legacy, and live life on purpose, not by conforming. And that is what this book is all about. If you are one of those Gen-X folks, or a Boomer, you really need to read this! If you are part of Gen-Y, then this insight will help you navigate your way to a purpose-filled life while funding it at the same time. It will give you freedom. It is not a typical how-to book; there is nothing typical about anything anymore. The book is more about the discovery, the widening of understanding, and the soul-searching exercise for the brand *you*.

It comes with some of my personal experiences as well as those of many other change agents who are writing, blogging, and giving some incredible insight into the new normal that we all must understand and participate in. Some of those change agents include names that you probably have heard of, such as Earl Nightingale, Jim Rohn, Seth Godin, Tony Robbins, Michael Gerber, Robert Kiyosaki, and Jack Canfield. A few may be new to you, but still change agents indeed: Jerry Clark, Simon Sinek, Scott Dinsmore, Jason Dorsey, Pamela Slim and Eric Worre. I hope that these insights that I present give you a road map for this new normal; a map for you to leave a legacy of your own; a way to not have any regrets when the clock stops ticking. I hope you enjoy and spread the word to others. My own personal legacy is what you are about to read.

Acknowledgements

I certainly would be remiss to not acknowledge my parents, Harvey D & Dorothy J Hess in Pittsburgh, PA for their wonderful job of raising six children who have all excelled in their lives. It is all about the love, the ethics, morals and integrity instilled upon us starting at a very young age.

And to my children, Tera, Heather and Bryan, who have those same values that were so instrumental in my upbringing.

And I gratefully acknowledge the many, many mentors that I have had the privilege of learning from—past, present, and I am sure, more in the future—since learning is, and should be, an ever occurring part of life. You will find many of those mentors within.

Introduction

"Don't Worry, Be Happy,"

– Bobby McFerrin

You have probably heard the term the "New Normal" at various times since our most recent economic recession. The "new normal" term has been used by the Wall Streeters when discussing the financial situation in the world; when describing the technology advances, and cyber-attacks that accompany it; when discussing globalization; and when discussing just about everything that has been changing these days, and which is a lot. Well the New Normal actually began in the 90s, and has been accelerating over the past decade. The new normal we are going to talk about are the changes within the job market and in earning an income.

Have you noticed the real changes that have occurred since the mid- to late-90s? The changes from an industrial society, which lasted for over 100 years, to a service society and a connection society, where everything is now different. Well, just about everything. The U.S. Bureau of Labor recently found that the average salary for college graduates in 2014 stands at just over $40,000 a year. Unfortunately, more than 50 percent of college graduates are either not working at all, working a part-time job, or working outside of their college degree. A popular axiom is that we now have the most educated waiters and bartenders in the world. We have retail bankers with little to no experience, but are cost effective; that we have thousands of people graduating from college each year with little chance to have a career like their parents, or especially their grandparents, had. These graduates do have one sure thing: a mountain of debt. And now even those parents and grandparents are under stress trying to figure out how to increase cash flow into, and through, retirement.

Why did this happen? Around the mid- to late-90s everything started to change. It became a more ruthless corporate environment, for sure:

caused by advanced technology, consolidation, globalization, and the power—and desire for—low-cost goods and services. It was caused by trying to squeeze every last ounce out of the capitalistic way of life we have developed for hundreds of years. It was the squeeze at the end of the Industrial Economy: the race to the bottom. And we have arrived.

Yes, there is a new normal. It is now not about really making much of anything, but more about how to provide service to others; the movement of money through providing a service; the movement of money through a more connected consumer base; and the movement of money by being well connected to things that shape a better life for others, or the perception of a better life. The new economy will be a real eye-opener for most. What we knew as "earning an income" by an hourly or salary job or by selling something, such as houses, cars or potato chips (my first job out of college) will be under increased pressure for the coming years. The new model for companies in paying wages in this new economy will be based more upon certain performance parameters, rather than just time for money or a commission for a one time sale.

The exponential rise in technology and efficiencies in the system has created more and more people available for the typical job. Being an employee of someone else, where you receive an IRS W-2 at year's end, will continue to be strained in wages versus the cost of living. Companies know that they have many more people to choose from and those are willing to do the work for less than what they were accustomed to paying. It will be a continual cycle, and will be based more upon performance than just raw numbers. In other words, your income, or potential income, will be based upon a set of factors upon which the company will decide, based upon how well the business performs. The possibility of making far less in one year than the next will be real. Trying to budget and live at the current standard of living in that income environment will be difficult for most, at best. This is the new normal.

For those paying attention, those who really understand some of the parameters of this new reality, the new normal will be more about finding what you are passionate about and then finding a Business Model that fits your passions, and allows you to maintain a standard of living which enables you to live a happy, healthy life while leaving a legacy for others. That is the reason you need this book: this will be your road map for this new normal society we have today, and for the foreseeable future.

Marketing guru Seth Godin, one of my favorite authors, marketers and trenders, states in his book *The Purple Cow* that we are all marketers now, that your products are either remarkable or invisible, that even if you are very good, that is fairly bad; that was over 13 years ago. In follow-up books over the past 12, like *The Tribe, Linchpin,* and *The Icarus Deception*, Mr. Godin describes this new normal in a human perspective: become a leader, no matter what it is you do, and become emotionally "all in" for your work and your career. It is about being an artist, not just a pawn on the board of life; if you are the pawn, then you have conformed. If you do not build your dream then someone will hire you to build their dream, but not at what you believe you are worth.

You will learn in this book that conformity is what has kept most people broke. Conformity is what we have been taught, all of us, everyone. But it is not what works in this new normal. As Mr. Godin says, "There are no longer any great jobs where someone else tells you precisely what to do." And not conforming is exactly that, being different. As he says in *Linchpin*: "You don't become indispensable merely because you are different. But the only way to become indispensable is to be different. That is because if you're the same, so are plenty of other people." This book is all about how to create a great life by not conforming. It will be all about finding what drives you and what your passions are, and then selecting the proper business idea and model that fits your passions, your mission, your values.

In obtaining a copy of this book, you now have, in a figurative way, insurance to help you safely and securely find your dream. Those who have not had this information may have already paid a heavy toll in money and time pursuing their dream with a faulty road map. I know: I have seen it many times in my career and in my early experiences, I, too, have suffered the same frustrations.

So many jobs have vanished—believe it or not, over 42,000 factories alone have closed in the U.S. in the past decade—that this "New Normal" is forcing individuals out of the easy solution of job-hunting, into a scarier proposition of really needing to figure out the what, where, and how to keep a roof over the family and food on the table. The effects of the global industrial economy, along with our 21st century economic system, which is heavily reliant upon cheap money; cheap energy, which is not cheap any longer; and ever-appreciating assets that have been depreciating for years now, is causing the average person some major reevaluations of how to create cash flow in their lives for themselves and their family. At the time of this writing Bankrate.com had just published a survey which found that roughly three quarters of the population in the U.S. is living paycheck-to-paycheck, with little to no emergency savings; and 27 percent have no savings at all. We now have the most people ever on Food Stamps, otherwise known now as the "'Supplemental Nutrition Assistance Program." And we are seeing a certain reduction of the typical standard of living for the middle class; a squeeze is upon us. Added to all of that is a Baby Boomer generation whose members are turning 65 years old at a rate of 10,000 people a day for the next 15 years.

It sounds like a perfect storm to me. It is this New Normal we will be discussing and, after you read this book, I promise with full confidence that you will be able to avoid heartache and expense as you make your choice of a business endeavor to secure a cash flow for your life. Your future can be virtually free of the headaches and frustrations and free of risking precious time and money in choosing a way to create an income that is right for you. That is my goal in writing this book.

This information is your private counselor: your consultant to help you navigate the turbulent waters of deciphering the real businesses from the quackery and scammers that float by us each day. It is an adviser that will allow you to decode whether your business idea has merit and fits some of the universal laws, such as the Law of Consumerism, which we will be discussing in detail in upcoming chapters. Although I could compose a list of ideas or companies with the Connection-Economy-likeness and offer my opinions on each of them, I would far rather share with you the formula for deciding this on your own. I would rather share with you how to fish, than give you a fish.

You will learn that the major "play" in this new economy is Network Marketing. It is a perfect solution at a perfect time in history for this type of Business Model. I am going to give you some of the reasons why this is by looking at some of the traditional Business Models under stress today and I will provide the information necessary to figure out Network Marketing, a very misunderstood Business Model and profession.

If you currently have a job, or go to work every day, and if it is something that you "have to do" instead of something you "get to do," and if your whole life feels like a job—something we do every day starting over again the next day, hoping Saturday or Sunday gets here fast—then this is a book for you. If you are one of those statistics above, with little-to-no savings and the inability to have a cushion in case of an emergency, then this book is for you. If you are one of those Baby Boomers out there not ready for the 20 or 30 years of maintaining a standard of living without productive employment and lack savings then this is for you. If you are currently unemployed, or underemployed, then this book is for you. If you are a part of Gen Y or Gen X and are not sure what legacy you will have on this earth, then this book is for you. An old saying states, "If you are not growing as a person, then you are dying a little every day"; human beings want the feeling of vitality, of growing, of being happy and having a fun, fulfilling life, without the stress of having enough money in savings, and so on. You can have that by deciding what drives you, with some consistent focus and action and the correct Business Model or idea. And with those three things, your life can change in a matter of minutes, not months or years.

As I mentioned before this is not your typical "how-to" book. I will give you some factors and some best-in-class modeling to look at when analyzing any career endeavor, but this is going to be an exercise in finding what makes you tick, what your real passions are in life. Many times, work is expending energy, or effort, on something we really do not want to do whereas passion is expending energy on the things we love to do. The goal is not simply to "work hard, play hard," which was one of the mantras of the Industrial Era; the goal is to make your work and your play indistinguishable. The goal is to find that passion within you, so you really never have to work again.

Maybe you have been thinking deeply about starting your own business, about getting out of the proverbial rat race, that your job is just that, a job. Maybe you have an idea, something that you can create but are not sure how to execute. Maybe you have been doing some searching, looking at potential offers to buy this business or franchise that business or looking to join a Network Marketing business opportunity or sign up as a sales representative of some product or service. Maybe you have this dream about working from home. New companies are popping up at a rate never before seen in the United

States, offering you the opportunity to work your way to financial freedom. The reason is simple: throughout the past 50 years, whenever the economy takes a downturn, Americans respond by seeking business opportunities. Americans are the most vibrant entrepreneurs on planet earth.

More really good news is now that we are in the worst economic downturn of the century, the start-your-own-business world is white hot. The spirit of American entrepreneurship is responding as it always has saying okay, "I have lost my job, so I will start my own business and not worry about downsizing again." It is not unusual that people want to own their own business, but it is easier today than at any time in history. This book is dedicated to helping you to navigate those confusing waters in which you must swim to make your decision.

You will be facing some fears along the way: maybe you have been thinking about making some kind of move for a while now, starting something, even part time, that can get you closer to your personal mission in life (if, that is, you have even thought about what your personal mission might be!) or maybe you have tried some type of business venture before, with poor results. You might be scared, you might be afraid to get out there, to put yourself out there, try again if that is the case. Well, having that fear is part of human nature but, speaking frankly, it says that you are gutless. Get over it. So much of starting a business or affecting change boils down to the confidence and courage to simply try. If you do not want to be one of the 75 percent living paycheck to paycheck then you must do something about it. Life leaves clues, and success leaves clues, all you need is the road map.

I hope you will end up with the map here. It is my desire, and resolve, to put something in people's hands that will assist them in making the right moves, while understanding themselves and throwing the cloak of fear off the back. It is getting started at something, and knowing, in your heart that it will change your life, and those lives you touch.

Another old saying claims that it is the start that stops most people. I heard it said a little differently recently, "you do not have to be great to start, but you have to start to be great." I want you to be great by following the advice in this book. I have full confidence in you.

Now for some good news and bad news. The good news is you have this book, and you are reading it. The bad news is that you may be reading this because you do not have the money, lifestyle, or personal fulfillment you want and dream about. The good news is that it is it is available to you and it is closer to you right now than you can believe. The bad news is there are a number of business ideas and Business Models out there that, though they will leave you frustrated and broke, they are wrapped in lovely paper and bows. The good news is there are some solid choices as well and places to get the information you need to decide if venturing out on your own is for you. The bad news is you need to make a proper and correct decision of which business idea or model to find and choose as the answer to your situation. The good news is this book will safely guide you to that objective.

Chapter 1

Why Listen To Me?

"Even if you're on the right track,
you will get run over if you just sit there."

– Will Rogers

Andrew Jackson once said, "Learn from the mistakes of others; we do not have enough time to make them all ourselves." So in this chapter I give you some of my triumphs and many mistakes. I hope you learn from them!

As we go through life we gain all kinds of experiences. Life itself is one big education, right? Well, I have lived a life with so many experiences that it kind of feels like multiple lives! I have had the pleasure to have traveled to and worked in over 50 countries thus far and all the U.S. States and Canadian provinces, save a few. I am well-versed in retail, franchising and product distribution, albeit most of which occurred in the old Industrial Economy. These experiences have been enough for several lifetimes, and I feel like I am just getting started.

Who am I? What do I think, and why? Before we get too far along, I think it is important for us to get acquainted. I know that you are a wise business person because you are willing to educate yourself so I know you want to know a little about me.

I did what I was supposed to do: I went to college and received a degree in Forestry, believe it or not. Then I went to work for a large convenience store chain, The Circle K Corporation. In all, I spent 20 years working to achieve my place as a successful leader in Corporate America as a Fortune 500 company executive and then another couple of years as an executive consultant. I had the paychecks, the benefits, the lifestyle and the respect. I flew about the U.S. and the world, managing hundreds of retail businesses holding titles like Director of Western

Region Operations, Director of Worldwide Franchise, and President of the International Division. I was, and still am, fairly well educated in product distribution, how products and services move through the supply chain to a customer. I am not sharing this to impress you, but to qualify me. I want to share the point that I had a career that we are taught to pursue as Americans: the American Dream.

I had the fictional creation of the "American Dream," not the real thing. What I had was certainly not dreamy: it was a high stress, high effort, albeit well paid career. I was owned: I was simply an organic asset of someone else's dream. I could not always be with my friends or family, my job was on the road, miles from home. At any moment I could have been fired, discarded without care or concern as I had seen happen to many others during my tenure.

As you read this, perhaps you are in a similar lifestyle and career, or you may be underemployed or unemployed. If you are the latter you may be tempted to say, "Wait, that is what I want, what you had! I want that title, that paycheck, that first class airplane ticket." I am here to tell you that it is not what you will really have once you have given 15 or 20 years to get there. I am here to tell you that you can have the same or better financial freedom accompanied by time and independence to be with your family, and do it in time measured in months, not decades. And I am here to tell you that basically, the old-style economy is gone and will never return. It is now all about being more connected and understanding this new normal, this new economy: it is all about being resourceful. No company, or anyone for that matter, is going to provide you with a great life.

In *The Icarus Deception,* Mr. Godin discusses how, throughout our entire lives, it has been about coordinating our comfort zone with our safety zone. With this New Economy, it has all changed. He goes on to say:

"The safety zone has changed, but your comfort zone has not. Those places that felt safe—the corner office, the famous college, the secure job—aren't. You are holding back, betting on a return to normal, but in the new normal, your resistance to change is no longer helpful.

"We made a mistake. We settled for a safety zone that was not bold enough and that embraced authority and compliance. We build our comfort zone around being obedient and invisible, and as a result, we are far too close to the waves.

"You can go to as many meetings, read as many books, and attend as many seminars as you like, but if you do not figure out how to realign your comfort zone with today's new safety zone, all the strategy in the world isn't going to help you."

At the risk of using a fairly well used cliché, I am inviting you to not only get out of the 40-40-40-40 plan, but to understand that for many, it is gone forever. I use this analogy because I had some 40's in my version. People today are often slaves to a 40-hour-a-week job that pays $40,000, and you retire with 40 percent of your income after 40 years of your life. I extend it out. For 40 years you will have less than 40 percent of your significant others life and presence around you; you will get a $40 engraved watch after all of those faithful years of service and effort, and finally the company you worked for will forget your name 40 days—or 40 minutes—after you leave. Besides, with the new normal upon us, those days are H-I-S-T-O-R-Y anyway! If you think that they are not, I am asking you to "get over it," they are D-O-N-E.

But where do you go? Want do you do? That was the question I had to answer: what was next in life and how do I support my family? Looking back at it today, I rather blindly started my own business, which ended up being multiple businesses! The first business I chose was to open an International Franchise and Retail Consulting Business. Being self-employed, from there it was investigating all kinds of small businesses, franchises, and home-based businesses.

I started to realize that to be happy, to feel fulfilled, you had to find something that you had some passion for, a reason why. I also started reading more business books and one in particular, changed everything for me. In late 2001, I picked up Robert Kiyosaki's *Cash Flow Quadrant*, the sequel to his best seller *Rich Dad Poor Dad.* I will never forget standing in a Barnes & Noble reading the book's back cover and it sang to me:

"It is a book written for...

- people who are ready to move beyond job security and begin to find their own world of financial freedom
- people who are ready to make deep professional and financial changes in their lives

- people who are ready to move from the industrial age to the information age

These quotes sealed it for me...

> "This book is about choosing new options, new directions, and a new financial future," said by Mr. Kiyosaki.
>
> "You cannot teach a person anything; you can only help him find it within himself," said by Galileo.
>
> "Many people will not head down the street until all the lights are green. That is why they do not go anywhere," said by Keith Cunningham, co-founder of Prime Cable.

I just had to read this book thoroughly! And I did, cover to cover, two or three times. I had more "Aha!" moments reading this one book than anything I had ever read before. I started to understand that I had just traded one "never get ahead financially and no time freedom job" as an employee working for someone else to another "never get ahead financially and no time freedom job" as a self-employed business owner! I no longer had any passion for either. Also, and I did not realize it at the time, the way of the past was but a fleeting moment; now the new age, which started to be called the "Information Age," a name that morphed into the Connection Economy, was just developing and I had a feeling.

Probably the most "Aha!" moment from the book was understanding the different ways to fund your life. I just had never really thought about the differences between "transactional income," or time for money, and "residual income," or utilizing leverage. It is interesting to note, as Mr. Kiyosaki points out, that "many of the brightest graduates from our universities want to work for college dropouts...dropouts like Bill Gates, Richard Branson, Michael Dell, and Ted Turner; dropouts who today are the mega-rich of society." In fact, his latest work, *Why "A" Students Work for "C" Students and Why "B" Students Work for the Government: Rich Dad's Guide to Financial Education for Parents* cuts right to the chase in this new normal we are now living in. This one is a must-read not only for parents but also for Generation Y.

Why, you might ask, is it all different and why are the college dropouts, or "C" students a success? One of the reasons is because they learned the importance of, and the difference between, transactional income, which is being an employee or being self-employed, compared to leveraged or residual income, which is being a true business owner. Many of us have the same goal in mind, financially speaking: to be an investor and allow our money to work for us, making money while we sleep, work, or vacation. They also understood the *why*, not just the *what*. It is the *why,* the vision and mission, that drives any and all successful companies or organizations. There is an old saying that goes like this: "The person who knows how will always have a job working for the person who knows why."

It was a total revelation for me!

So, I began to search for my passion, what did I love to do? If money was no object, what would I be doing every day? I jumped into the world of Internet Marketing, Internet Shopping, and Health and Wellness. Why? Because it was something I knew a bit about, I liked it, and I saw an avenue to help others looking to transition at the same time. I found that I really enjoyed helping others succeed, loved to be a part of it all.

However, I learned something very important during this time of starting a new company, as an Independent Contractor, utilizing the Network Marketing Business Model with an MLM compensation structure. I will cover these in Chapters 10 and 11.

I used to talk all the time about the freedom of creating a true, long term residual income and the idea that everyone should have every day be like Saturday. I talked about it so much that I named my company, Everyday's a Saturday, LLC (www.EverydaysASaturday.com) and a friend sent me an email that summed up my idea:

> *The older I get, the more I enjoy Saturday mornings. Perhaps it's the quiet solitude that comes with being the first to rise, or maybe it's the unbounded joy of not having to be at work. Either way, the first few hours of a Saturday morning are most enjoyable.*
>
> *A few weeks ago, I was shuffling toward the kitchen with a steaming cup of coffee in one hand and the morning paper in the other. What began as a typical Saturday morning turned into one of those lessons that life seems to hand you from time to time. Let me tell you about it.*

I turned the volume up on my radio in order to listen to a Saturday morning talk show. I heard an older sounding gentleman with a golden voice. You know the kind, he sounded like he should be in the broadcasting business. He was telling whoever he was talking with something about "a thousand marbles."

I was intrigued and sat down to listen to what he had to say.

"Well, Tom, it sure sounds like you're busy with your job. I'm sure they pay you well, but it's a shame you have to be away from home and your family so much. Hard to believe a young fellow should have to work sixty or seventy hours a week to make ends meet. Too bad you missed your daughter's dance recital." He continued, "Let me tell you something Tom, something that has helped me keep a good perspective on my own priorities."

And that is when he began to explain his theory of "a thousand marbles."

"You see, I sat down one day and did a little arithmetic. The average person lives about seventy-five years. I know, some live more and some live less, but on average, folks live about seventy-five years.

"Now, I multiplied 75 times 52, and I came up with 3900, which is the number of Saturdays that the average person has in their entire lifetime.

"Now stick with me Tom, I'm getting to the important part.

"It took me until I was fifty-five years old to think about all this in any detail," he went on, "and by that time I had lived through over twenty-eight hundred Saturdays. I got to thinking that if I lived to be seventy-five, I only had about a thousand of them left to enjoy.

"So I went to a toy store and bought every single marble they had. I ended up having to visit three toy stores to roundup 1000 marbles. I took them home and put them inside of a large, clear plastic container right here in the shack next to my gear. Every Saturday since then, I have taken one marble out and thrown it away.

"I found that by watching the marbles diminish, I focus more on the really important things in life. There is nothing like watching

your time here on this earth run out to help get your priorities straight.

"Now let me tell you one last thing before I sign-off with you and take my lovely wife out for breakfast. This morning, I took the very last marble out of the container. I figure if I make it until next Saturday then God has blessed me with a little extra time to be with my loved ones.

"It was nice to talk to you Tom. I hope you spend more time with your loved ones, and I hope to meet you again someday. Have a good morning!"

You could have heard a pin drop when he finished. Even the show's moderator didn't have anything to say for a few moments. I guess he gave us all a lot to think about.

I had planned to do some work that morning, then go to the gym. Instead, I went upstairs and woke my wife up with a kiss. "C'mon honey, I'm taking you and the kids to breakfast."

"What brought this on?" she asked with a smile. "Oh, nothing special," I said. "It's just been a long time since we spent a Saturday together with the kids. Hey, can we stop at a toy store while we're out? I need to buy some marbles."

This story really got to me. I cried when I read it. I cried when I recited it for this chapter. I still cry every time I read it.

Tiptoeing through life to arrive at your grave safely, or really, really, creating a life of purpose, with emotional joy and freedom. That is the ultimate life question!

There is a fine line between attempting to secure your financial and time freedom future and keep the lights on and food on the table; a fine line between self employment and unemployment. It is why so many marriages end in divorce, one person chasing the dream, the other frustrated with the insecurity of it all: the fear of failure, the fear of embarrassment with friends and family, the fear of an uncertain future. You see, it is much easier to just go to work somewhere, put in your hours, collect the paycheck, keep the wife and children happy, and pay the bills. An acquaintance of mine, Jerry Clark, calls it "tiptoeing through life to arrive at your grave safely." It is a decision, one that people make every single day. Venture out to be an entrepreneur or choose the safety net of an employee-company relationship. Transactional vs. leverage/residual income, that is the decision you should be able to make by the end of this book.

And hopefully, if you decide on the latter, this book will give you the insight, the how-to, the ability to shake the cloak of fear off your back and then never look back.

In the past 36 years I have transitioned from a Corporate Executive to a Traditional Small Business owner to a Professional Network Marketer. I am passionate in helping others make the transition, too; the timing is perfect, right now.

Chapter 2

The New Normal, The Connection Economy

"The only thing we have to fear is fear itself."

– Franklin Delano Roosevelt

We live in a performance society, nothing like the old Industrial Economy. In his latest book, *The Icarus Deception*, marketing guru Seth Godin makes the case for approaching work as art. In this excerpt, which I consider one of the best explanations of our economy today, he explains how we are living in an economy that rewards achievement and connection instead of compliance:

> *The value we create is directly related to how much valuable information we can produce, how much trust we can earn, and how often we innovate.*
>
> *In the industrial economy, the stuff we made (literally stuff—widgets, devices, and O-rings) comprised the best assets we could build. Fortunes belonged to men who built railroads, light bulbs, and buildings. Today we're seeking something a revolution apart from that sort of productivity.*
>
> *The connection economy rewards the leader, the initiator, and the rebel. The internet wasn't built to make it easy for you to watch Lady Gaga videos. The internet is a connection machine, and anyone with a laptop or a smartphone is now connected to just about everyone else.*
>
> *And it turns out that those connections are changing the world. If your factory burns down but you have loyal customers, you'll be fine. On the other hand, if you lose your customers, even*

> *your factory isn't going to help you—Detroit is filled with empty factories.*
>
> *If your team is filled with people who work for the company, you'll soon be defeated by tribes of people who work for a cause.*
>
> *If you use your money to buy advertising to promote the average products you produce for average people, soon you'll run out of money. But if you use your money to make exceptional products and services, you won't need to spend it on advertising, because your customers will connect to one another and bring you more.*
>
> *The connection economy has changed how you get a job and what you do when you get to that job. It has changed how we make and listen to music, write and read books, and discover where to eat, what to eat, and whom to eat with.*
>
> *It has destroyed the mediocre middle of average products for average people who have few choices, and it has enabled the weird edges, where people who care find others who care and they all end up caring about something even more than they did before they met.*
>
> *The connection economy enables endless choice and endless shelf space and puts a premium on attention and on trust, neither of which is endless.*
>
> *Most of all, the connection economy has made competence not particularly valuable and has replaced it with an insatiable desire for things that are new, real, and important.*

Wow! Very, very insightful, right? The new normal, this Connection Economy, is only in its infancy. It has really just started, maybe 10 years or so ago. That is why so many of us who have been the conformist with society and our economy have not yet fathomed what is happening. It is why I have talked to people every single week who are struggling to understand what is going on around them, who are wondering what it means to them, what they may bring, in the form of value, to the marketplace, especially if they are the currently unemployed or underemployed. It is especially happening with the young at heart, the members of Gen-Y who have been sold a bill of goods from our universities that everything continues to be as it has always been. Our universities are still focused on churning out employees with no teaching about finances, how money works, or our changing society and economy. Unless you are going to be a specialist in a field, like a brain surgeon, then in my opinion the only thing our universities have given those in the past 10–15 years is a mountain of debt. It will take the imaginative mind, the person who really gets what is going on today, does not conform, that does not become complacent, that does not hope that things change to the way they were. It will be the person with some new business ideas, or a better way to bring trust and service to the marketplace, that will get out there, connect, make something happen.

It will be people like Mark Levine and Michael Dubin, founders of Dollar Shave Club, www.dollarshaveclub.com, who in 2011 turned the razor blade industry upside down. I cannot count how many times over the past 20 or 30 years or longer that I was totally frustrated with the razor blade industry. As one of those "needed" consumer goods, the razor industry has been controlled by just two companies, Gillette, owned by Procter & Gamble, and Schick, owned by Energizer Holdings. Control means owning the retail space, owning the distribution, and setting the prices for razors and blades that reward the shareholders within that company. I mean, really, $34 for 6 or 8 razor blades? Give me a break. What do you think they cost to make those things in China? Maybe 80 cents or so. Then, as part of this new Connection Economy, here comes Dollar Shave Club, connecting people via word-of-mouth, social media, blogs, and general mayhem, to this great idea, join the club: get five cartridges for $1 a month! Yes, $1. Now, for $12 a year, I can replace my blades once a week and not get cut; I was always so reluctant to change out the Gillette blades for months because the cost would drive me batty!

The new economy is like this eclectic, hip place that opened in Phoenix, Arizona called The Duce. A couple of ex-business owners from Chicago, Steve and Andi Rosenstein, sold their business, moved to Scottsdale, retired, got bored, and decided to try something totally different: enter The Duce. They bought an old warehouse in Phoenix which now offers, among other amenities, a restaurant, full bar, gym with a complete boxing ring, coffee bar, old-fashioned soda fountain, fresh organic produce stand, and retro clothing and collectibles that the Rosensteins have gathered from around the country and Europe. It is not one of your stamp-it-out chain-type gyms and restaurants; it is totally the new economy.

The new Connection Economy is Amazon, Netflix, Tesla, Instagram, Uber, Airbnb; they are all about getting closer to the customer, more direct, cutting out the waste, utilizing technology. It is why the Network Marketing profession is booming, too.

If you really want to get an up close and personal look at this new, growing Connection Economy, visit Scott Dinsmore's Live Your Legend website and blog, www.liveyourlegend.net. Mr. Dinsmore highlights all kinds of folks living their passion while he is doing the same, at 32 years old! You can also download from his site for free a 27-question workbook about finding your passion. We will be discussing passion, your why, and your purpose as we move through the book. Definitely worth a look! It is what this new Connection Economy is all about.

However, the new connection economy is no different than the old Industrial Economy in two ways. First, you have to understand that it will always be about being well prepared and working hard – really hard – to succeed (especially as an entrepreneur). Second, the need to monetize the new business, new idea, or new partnership with a network marketing company to fulfill every day necessities and obligations are still there. If you are thinking about opening your own business, traditional brick and mortar or out of your home, then you will first want to read Michael Gerber's *The E-Myth Revisited.*

As we will be talking about living a more purposeful life and living your passion, you must also understand that running a business because you are passionate about doing something (for example, cutting hair as a cosmetologist) and running a hair salon are two entirely different things. The most important factor, and one we discuss here, is to study Business Models and trends; learn to work on your business, not in your business.

I have a classic story to illustrate my point. Years ago my wife was itching to do something and decided upon a career in cosmetology. Off to cosmetology school she went and then, for the next four or five years, worked in a salon cutting, coloring, and all the other activities that go on in hair salons. One day, she came home and said that the local salon, within walking distance to our house, was for sale. She wanted to buy it and open her own salon. Knowing right away that owning and running a business and working as a stylist in that business were two entirely different things, I started asking questions about whether she had thought about a business plan, if she was going to hire a manager, how she was going to structure the business, what the proforma stated the monthly and yearly results would be, and how much in startup and working capital she would need to get things up and running.

Obviously, these were questions she had not even begun to think about, but the idea of walking to her own salon, cutting and coloring for her clients, and all the fun stuff that goes along with that almost had her jumping off the bridge, so to speak. We never did buy that salon.

I have seen it over and over and over again in my life: people enamored with their own business, but not understanding how to work on their business, not just in it. In fact, that salon in my neighborhood has turned over at least eight times in the past 18 years, amazing. So the *E-myth Revisited* is an excellent starting point for those thinking about being an entrepreneur. The second factor is the funding of one's life with money—which is the way of the land—that becomes important to all. Money. If you have some kind of emotional attachment to money, or lack of it, then that one issue will stand in the way for you, forever. Unless you change your thoughts and your ideas about money. There are numerous people out there today thinking they will create a continual, lifelong income by blogging, or coming up with a new mobile app, or various other new economy ideas. Unfortunately, it is not always that simple.

Finding a way to create cash flow and to live your passion is all about the right business idea and model, getting ahead of the trends, utilizing leverage, and a duplicatable process that will deliver to you the money you need to live a fulfilling life. The amount needed is different for everyone, depending upon goals, wants, needs, desires, and giving back. Money. Let us get straight and right about money right now. Here is some more insight from Seth Godin on a recent blog posting about money:

A few things to keep in mind:

1. *The amount of money you have has nothing to do with whether or not you're a good person. Being good with money is a little like being good with cards. People who are good at playing cards*

aren't better or worse than anyone else, they're just better at playing crazy eights.

2. *Money spent on one thing is still the same as money spent on something else. A $500 needless fee on a million-dollar mortgage closing is just as much money as a $500 tip at McDonald's.*
3. *If you borrow money to make money, you have done something magical. On the other hand, if you go into debt to pay your bills or buy something you want but do not need, you have done something stupid. Stupid and short-sighted and ultimately life-changing for the worse.*
4. *To go along with #3: getting out of debt as fast as you possibly can is the smartest thing you can do with your money. If you need proof to confirm this, ask anyone with money to show you the math. Hint: credit card companies make more profit than just about any other companies in the world.*
5. *There's no difference (in terms of the money you have) between spending money and not earning money, no difference between not-spending money and getting a raise (actually, because of taxes, you're even better off not-spending). If you have got cable TV and a cell phone, you're spending $4,000 a year, $6,000 before taxes.*
6. *If money is an emotional issue for you, you have just put your finger on a big part of the problem. No one who is good at building houses has an emotional problem with hammers. Place your emotional problems where they belong, and focus on seeing money as a tool.*
7. *Like many important, professional endeavors, money has its own vocabulary. It won't take you long to learn what opportunity cost, investment, debt, leverage, basis points, and sunk costs mean, but it'll be worth your time.*
8. *Never sign a contract or make an investment that you do not understand at least as well as the person on the other side of the transaction.*
9. *If you've got a job, a steady day job, now's the time to figure out a way to earn extra income in your spare time. Freelancing, selling items on EBay, building a side business—two hundred*

extra dollars every week for the next twenty years can create peace of mind for a lifetime.

10. *The chances that a small-time investor will get lucky by timing the stock market or with other opaque investments are slim, fat, and none.*
11. *The way you feel about giving money to good causes has a lot to do with the way you feel about money.*
12. *Don't get caught confusing money with security. There are lots of ways to build a life that's more secure, starting with the stories you tell yourself, the people you surround yourself with, and the cost of living you embrace. Money is one way to feel more secure, but money alone won't deliver this.*
13. *Rich guys busted for insider trading weren't risking everything to make more money for the security that money can bring. In fact, the very opposite is starkly shown here. The insatiable need for more money is directly (and ironically) related to not being clear about what will ultimately bring security. Like many on this path, now they have neither money nor security.*
14. *In our culture, making more money feels like winning, and winning feels like the point.*
15. *Within very wide bands, more money does not make people happier. Learning how to think about money, though, usually does.*
16. *In the long run, doing work that is important leads to more happiness than doing work that is merely profitable.*

The last point, doing work that is important leads to more happiness than doing work that is merely profitable, is the absolute truism about money. Do you think that the 80 percent of respondents to a recent survey who said they hated their jobs hated it because of the money? Probably not. Anyone can find a job that will, for the most part, pay the bills. It is finding joy in what you do that will eventually win out. And, because of the way society works, it takes a way to fund it with money that has to work in conjunction with the joy, the passion, the purpose.

So this new economy will be one for those who think. It will take thinking, problem-solving, earning trust, using the social connection network, and doing it on purpose and with passion. Is that you? Read on and see.

Chapter 3

Do You Know Why?

"Some men see things as they are and say, 'Why?'
I dream things that never were and say, 'Why not?'"

– George Bernard Shaw

There is an old saying: "The person who knows how will always have a job working for the person who knows why."

There is another old saying that "When the why is big enough, the how becomes easy."

And Mark Twain once famously said, "The two most important days in your life are the day you were born and the day you find out why."

A *why* is the gasoline in our entrepreneur motor. It is the discomfort and frustration we have that makes us get up and do things we regularly would not do. What is your *why* that drives you to seek success, money, and time freedom? If you do not have one, if you are not driven each day by a powerful *why*, then you have settled in some obscure village of compromise. I believe this is not the case, though, for those souls without a *why* would have already put this book down and would not have read this far.

Simon Sinek, in his powerful book *Start With Why* explains that literally no successful individual, no successful company, small or large, or movement, has ever been accomplished without the owner/leader/founder/CEO, knowing exactly *why* it is what it is. Sam Walton built an empire on a very strong *why*. The biggest challenge Wal*Mart has had since the passing of the visionary Mr. Walton in 1992 has been someone to carry on his vision, his *why*. It has not happened, and Mr. Walton would roll over in his grave if he saw what has become of Wal*Mart today, which is one of the most vilified companies in the history of commerce. At the time of this writing Wal*Mart was fighting massive amounts of lawsuits, individual and class action, and 199,000,000 Internet impressions, many of which are not favorable articles or information about Wal*Mart. However, it was not that way for Wal*Mart when Mr. Walton was alive. He understood the *why* behind Wal*Mart.

It is an incredible vision, a strong *why*, which will drive you to success in anything you take on in life. Martin Luther King had no idea how to make the idea of equality come to fruition, but he had a vision, an incredible 'why', which he spoke of in his "I Have a Dream" speech in 1963. Dr. King's *why* changed the world.

Achievement happens when we pursue and attain what we want. Success comes when we are in clear pursuit of why we want it.

If you are currently employed or underemployed but pining for more, if you are struggling with your own business currently, or if you are just wondering how to increase your cash flow, then I have one simple question, a question I heard from young Scott Dinsmore of Live Your Legend (www.liveyourlegend.net) : *Why do you do what you do?*

Think about it, deeply. Why do you do what you do? If the answer to that question is not that you absolutely, unequivocally love what you do, that you impact so many others, that you are leaving a legacy, that it fits your purpose and passion in life, then ask yourself again, why do you do what you do? It is a simple question, can you answer it?

What was my *why*? I wanted to own my life, my dream, and my time with friends and family, and I wanted to leave a legacy when my time here on earth was complete. Each time I departed for another airport, I was leaving my wife and children; there were no options to take them with me. To me, the American dream was to be with my wife, to be with my kids, not to be with the corporation that employed me. All of the praise for accomplishment, all of the money and perks that come with executive success are of little real value if in their attainment they rust the relationships you need for true fulfillment; the relationships you have with friends, with family, and the legacy you leave.

I believe we all have a *purpose* in life, a reason we were put on this earth. Our time here is rather short, if you really think about it, so what *purpose* do you have here? What will the dash between your beginning and end really mean? What will people remember you for? What is your *why*? I do not know what your *why* is, unless we are personally acquainted, but I can tell you that if you do not find it, sooner or later it will look back at you in the form of regret for things that could have been. Find it, then believe in it. We will talk more about belief in the next chapter.

Most of the people I have worked with over the years have had the same primary why that we are discussing now: more money, more time to use and spend it, and a less stressful environment to do it in.

I am asking you to discover and do what inspires you! I am asking you to surround yourself with like-minded, passionate people! I am asking you to really do that personal evaluation, especially as it relates to those with whom you currently surround yourself. Business coach and philosopher Jim Rohn once said that you are the average of the five people you spend the most time with. In a way, our frustrations and our life are best identified by the people who are causing it in the first place, good or bad. Here is a story that illustrates that point:

> *A new junior executive was hired just out of college. He had his degree in marketing and was excited to land his first job with a well-known and respected company. On Friday of his first work week, a long black limousine pulled up in front of his branch office. The driver came in and asked for "the new guy."*
>
> *"The owner of the corporation would like to take you to eat. Please come with me," he told the nervous man.*
>
> *"What an honor," thought the young man as he walked to the opened door of the limo. After an elegant lunch, the owner had the driver take a brief detour back to the office, stopping on a hillside where mansions were being built.*
>
> *Placing his hand on the shoulder of the young man, and holding his cigar in the other hand he gestured over the hillside panorama. "Can you imagine a beautiful home right there young man? Can you envision the white pillared front porch and the rock fence?"*
>
> *"Oh yes sir," he eagerly replied.*
>
> *"Can you stretch your imagination to see the huge barn that contains a car collection, and can you see horses running in the fenced in pasture to the right? It is all beautiful!"*

> *"Oh yes, sir. I see it, I see it," the young executive excitedly responded.*
>
> *"Well son, you work hard and be dedicated to this company. I want you to come in early and go home late. Burn that candle at both ends and in the middle when necessary. Do it for the next twenty years as you build your career and someday...someday, all that you see will be mine!"*

This was my reality—I was building another person's dream. After enough sleepless nights of frustration, I began searching for a way to create or find my *why*, my dream. I investigated hundreds of small business possibilities, including many home based businesses. In my search, I ran into my fear: the fear of following a wrong path or wrong plan. The fear of being seen as a failure; you know, the ego at work. I was fearful of not being able to provide, not being seen any longer as a good husband and father. My, oh my, did the fears emerge!

I tested the water several times with Network Marketing companies, who, on the surface looked legitimate. I began to learn the hard way that I could not just choose a path by the neon lights that advertise it. I found out that I could not judge a cake by its appearance—one taste told me that no matter how it looked, if the frosting on the cake was made with salt instead of sugar, I would be sorely disappointed, and several times I was.

Today, thousands of fly-by-night schemes and scams exist. All of them are cakes that may be richly decorated, but lack the proper ingredients necessary for you to guarantee your security and success. Some of the companies I tested the water on simply had poor management. Others had inferior, overpriced products and still others were presided over by unscrupulous individuals. It is painful and costly to prove the old adage that "if it sounds too good to be true, it usually is."

The frosting on these cakes is well placed advertising, enticing and inviting; and, depending on where you are in your life and career, you will be tempted as I was to jump in only to learn you may have made a mistake. Many times, this is due to making an emotional decision, not a real solid look under the covers business decision. Looking back, I can say that at least I was making a decision. Decision is the spark that ignites action. Until a decision is made, nothing happens, good or bad. If I would have had a counselor or a book, a list of items to check out before I entered the world of running my own business, I would have saved thousands of hours and dollars. I would have achieved my freedom faster and avoided many sleepless nights.

Get a bit of education, then make a decision, by following your *why*.

In *Start With Why,* Mr. Sinek gives us three very simple strategies to define our why:

> **1. Clarity**: You have to know 100 percent why you are making a move to a new company, opening a traditional business, or starting a Network Marketing business in the first place. And it really must be something that moves you.
>
> Saying, "I want to be rich," or, "To make more money," is not the real why, no way. Take some time to ask yourself deeper questions. What does becoming rich mean to you? Define it. How much more money do you want to make, and what are you going to do with it? Money is always the vehicle to something far more important. So it takes some real clarity to recognize what is it you really, really want to accomplish with more money.
>
> **2. How**: People who jump from job to job, company to company, system to system, or income stream to income stream do so because they do not have the clarity of their why. But once you have the clarity, then you have to know how you are going to reach your why. It is something much deeper; your values and principles.
>
> The how is the vehicle you chose to reach your why. However, in most cases, because we do not fully understand our why, we use the wrong vehicle to try and reach our destination. Whatever business you start, or company, organization, team, or system you use to reach your why, it must be in alignment with your personal values and principles. When we are trying to reach our why, while going against our internal compass, then we shut down. When you realize you are in the wrong environment, your dreams slowly become crushed. In most cases we do not realize we are in

the wrong environment until we have clarity of our why.

3. What: Once you have clarity of your why, and know how you are going to reach it, then you have to look at what others see. Your why is the belief you have for accomplishing something bigger than yourself. Your how is the actions you are taking daily to reach your why. But if people do not see that what you are saying and doing is in alignment, and consistent, then you will not reach your why. People will not be attracted to you, your energy will not be in alignment. I have seen this so many times with Network Marketing representatives who say that they are all about helping others succeed, but yet their actions are in alignment with just themselves. They are really all about themselves: about themselves making money, about themselves receiving all the recognition, about their ego. It is not in alignment with what they say outwardly, and is recognized easily by others.

So, take time today to get real clarity on what your true driving force is in succeeding with a business idea. Once you have figured out your real why, ask yourself this one very important question: "If money was not a concern, what would you want to do on a daily basis to fulfill your why?" Then find an income opportunity that will allow you to enjoy your passions while fulfilling your why!

And if you can't find the right income opportunity, create it!

Another way to really look at your *why*, your purpose, to live the life of your dreams, is to look at your default future. If you are employed or underemployed currently, if you are earning a living but not really living a great life, if you have too much month at the end of the money and never seem to get ahead, then I would invite you to look closely at your default future. Your default future is your future one, two, five, ten years from now if you do nothing. You may be able to continue on—with only the uncertainty of Corporate America and the new performance wage system I would be concerned about how long—but if you did, what does that look like? This is your default future, your future if you do nothing. If you continue to do what it is you are doing, but expect some different kind of result, or more money, more time or more freedom and so on well, that is known as the definition of insanity: doing the same thing over and over again but expecting different results.

I once heard a speaker say, "Why not me, and why not now?" When he made the decision, he went from being an immigrant from Mexico washing dishes and living in a small apartment with four or five others to earning over $1 million a year, in less than 24 months! Why not you, and why not now?

My own personal difficulty in getting a handle on my *why*, my purpose, and finding the correct vehicle that aligns with my values has passed though, and I now enjoy the success that I have always wanted. My company, Everydays A Saturday, (www.EverydaysASaturday.com) has been aligned with a Network Marketing company for over 10 years now. I saw the trends outlined in this book coming, and never worried about dealing with the ignorance that comes with being on the front end of new ways of business. I have been educating and assisting others to find their passion, their why, and changing their quality of life.

Each month my life gets better, my income increases, I am totally free to create my day, and my personal mission is a reality. I get up when my eyes open now and each and every day my job description is to do exactly what I want to do. I can take a vacation without worrying about taking months after it is over to pay for it—diminishing the memory of my trip. In fact, now when I escape for a week or two, I return to find I have made money while I was gone. I found my why, defeated my fears, and I am sharing my journey to help others. I love my life today and my *why*; my purpose now is to help as many others achieve their purpose while I am still here. I am so fortunate to sit on the Board of Directors of two non-profit organizations, assist another monthly, and am in a chapter of Rotary International. I would like the dash to say about Harvey Hess that "he was a man of honor and integrity, always giving of his time and money in the pursuit of helping others, living his life just like he said he would, with real purpose."

What was my fear? Perhaps it was self inspired prediction; I was afraid I would pick a business to start or own an enterprise and, in innocent ignorance, pick something that was destined to fail. Well, that fear manifested itself and that is what happened. A well-used acronym for FEAR is False Expectations Appearing Real. How true that is. What we fear the most is fear itself. But what do we really have to fear? Many people starting their own business, especially if it is one with a connection, word-of-mouth, or a referral marketing system fear asking others to help them, to see the information, and to try whatever it is they are selling. They become frozen, fearing what their friends, family, or acquaintances will think of them. Well, I love to remind those I am mentoring what former first lady Eleanor Roosevelt once said, "You would not worry so much about what others think of you if you realized how seldom they do." I mean, really, do you really think people are sitting around thinking about you? Maybe your mom and dad are thinking about you, once in a while, but no one else is. Everyone is so preoccupied with their own lives, their own business, and their own day-to-day activities that believe me, they are not thinking about you. So to worry about what others may be thinking is stinkin' thinkin' at best. Get over it.

Life really does leave clues. Success really does leave clues. With this new normal we have today, with the Connection Economy, those who really get it, jump on the right idea that they are passionate about, at the right time, tune into trends and what is going on, they will be the ones written about years from now. It can be you. This new normal is relatively new, only a decade or so old, and there are so many ways to participate, to bring value to the market, to be of value yourself, and to facilitate trust.

If you have heard the statement that "ignorance is bliss," you really know that ignorance is not bliss; ignorance is pain, ignorance will cost you. And fear manifests itself with a lack of knowledge, with lack of information, or education, or passion, belief. When you have confidence, you know where you are going and how you are getting there, and fear disappears. Be confident!

Want to do the exercises necessary to find your passion, your why? Go to www.liveyourlegend.net and get your totally free, 27-question to find your passion workbook.

So we have found our passion and our *why* and identified our fears; so what is next?

If you are not involved in your own business, chances are you have considered it. Perhaps it was someone you know who ventured out on their own who approached you with a DVD to watch at home, or a polite invitation to attend a presentation. Maybe you looked at all the different Franchise Businesses out there, or saw a small business for sale, and started dreaming about being an owner yourself. Do you have an idea for a business today? Something you have been thinking about?

Many people have had the thought, sometimes just a passing thought, sometimes a dream, other times a calling, to do something, anything, other than what they are doing.

If you went to a business overview, you were impressed with the excitement you saw in the faces of the presenters and the stories; you found it hard to believe the testimonial of certain individuals living "the life that most people only dream about."

You said "no" and thanked your friend for the invitation, but that night, maybe you found yourself wishing you could have the success you saw but just could not see yourself in that winning picture. If this has happened to you, you are not alone; you are part of tens of thousands who wish for, dream about, and want the lifestyle that you saw, but are stuck in their 9 to 5 jobs at worst. At best they are successful but burning their candles at both ends to support and sustain the dream. As I mentioned earlier, in a recent survey, 80 percent of the people working said that they really do not like their job! What a way to go through life!

Sadly, the truth of the matter is that in life, you are either building your dream, or you are part of the group that is building someone else's success. If you have not experienced this yet in your quest for self-business-determination, you will.

So my story is one of those success stories you have heard, I know. The difference between my story and the story you will create for yourself is that I am outlining the list of things you can do to avoid the pitfalls I had to work through. In this book and the series of ongoing blogs on the website (www.EverydaysASaturday.com) you will have a guide to allow you to find the company that will be there long after you have achieved your dreams. Here you will learn how to find and pick the business that will not be a casualty or statistic of failure but instead a long term successful partnership.

When the why is big enough, the how becomes easy. Stop right here for a bit, take an emotional break, stretch, get out a piece of paper and a pen, jot down the very first thing that comes to you: what would you be doing right now if money was plentiful? Work on your *why*.

Chapter 4

Start with Belief

"What we can or cannot do, what we consider possible or impossible, is rarely a function of our true capability. It is more likely a function of our beliefs about who we are."

– Tony Robbins

Belief is truly one of the most important words in the human language. There are so many 'believe it and you will achieve it' statements over the course of time that it would be hard to even list them all here. So many originate in the number one selling book of all time, the Bible, that we sometimes just become numb to the words. I am an amateur in the Bible, but you can pick out so many statements in that book that you just have to think about it all. Belief comes from many internal factors. Believe it or not, it starts at a very young age, almost before you can even speak!

Throughout our life we are bombarded with communication, both verbal and nonverbal, that begins to develop a belief system. Our belief system is what drives us and our decisions, it is how we think and what we think about, and it is virtually the whole story, the whole enchilada, as to whether you will live the life your desire or will be stuck. Sometimes, many times, your conscious thinking does not even have any control over your beliefs; its subconscious, or unconscious thinking. Scientist have come to the conclusion that basically all decisions that we make are made within seconds, and our conscious thought has nothing to do with it. I know, that is a scary thought. It is one that is extremely difficult for our conscious, thinking mind to wrap our heads around.

Throughout our upbringing, we are bombarded with what become erroneous paradigms, things that are said to us, sometimes over and over again which within our subconscious mind, become a true or believable statement and, thus, become part of our makeup. I remember when growing up as the oldest of six children—five of us boys (and to this day I feel bad for my sister!)—my father (a hard-working, self-made man) used to say to us, "No, you can't have that. What do you think, money grows on trees?" I cannot count how many times over my childhood I heard the statement that we couldn't afford to get a new ball, fishing pole, or some other device because money did not grow on trees. Our subconscious mind, over a period of time, recognizes that money must be very hard to obtain; that money is scarce. Our subconscious does not recognize what is real from not real. This is why you can probably complete these sentences, and why for some of us, our subconscious still believes some of these to be true. Try it for yourself. Can you complete these sentences?

- It is lonely at the _________.
- Some people are just in the right place ________________.
- Filthy _________.
- Money does not grow ___________________.

You see, your subconscious mind, your belief system, puts a block on any information contrary to what you have been told throughout life. And it is this block managed by your reticular activating system that does not allow outside stimuli to get through if it believes that it does not serve a purpose for you, based upon your belief system.

In his book *The Biology of Belief: Unleashing the Power of Consciousness*, cell biologist Bruce Lipton reported that the subconscious mind is processing some 20,000,000 environmental stimuli per second versus 40 environmental stimuli interpreted by our conscious minds in the same second. Ap Dijksterhuis and Loran Nordgren of the University of Amsterdam demonstrated the power of subconscious thinking in their research indicating that our conscious thought is constrained by the low capacity of our consciousness; subconscious thought does not have this constraint because the subconscious has a much higher capacity. It follows that conscious thought, by necessity, will often take into account a subset of the information it should take into account. So, basically what that means is we run on subconscious programs, not conscious thought. We make decisions sometimes within milliseconds based upon a set of beliefs that we have stored in our subconscious.

Let me give you a few examples. Say you are walking down the street with your significant other and you decide to get something to eat. You come up to two restaurants and you see that one restaurant is empty, while the other has a group of people laughing and conversing and eating. About six milliseconds into that scenario, your decision on which restaurant to visit was already made, and it had nothing to do with conscious thought. It had everything to do with social proof, one of the automatic programs we have in our subconscious. Social proof is to do what others are doing, in this case that it must be socially acceptable to be in the restaurant where others are and there must be something wrong with the one without people.

In another example of how our subconscious works, I was told about a movie a few years ago. The friend who told me about the movie said, "You are going to cry your eyes out." She knows that I can be a rather emotional being. About a year later while channel surfing one evening, I came across that movie and, having never seen it, thought it was a good time to watch. I said to myself, however, "I'm going to show my friend. There is no way I'm going to cry during this movie, I'm just not going to do it."

What do you think happened? That is right, about three-fourths of the way through I found myself crying, and crying and crying. Why? Because it is not my conscious mind or my conscious thinking and decision making that is in control of my emotional being. It is all subconscious, based up many, many different programs, beliefs, mindsets, and convictions all gathered in our mind, and we have little control over it. To get a little technical here: it is our limbic brain, the center portion which controls all of our decision making and all of our feelings, but has no capacity for communication. If you have ever made a decision because it just felt right, then that is your limbic brain at work.

So, what does this have to do with running a successful business, about the rest of your life? Everything!

All of these erroneous paradigms can be a detriment to success. I have actually seen adults sabotage their careers because as they advanced through Corporate America, for example, their belief system did not believe they were worthy of the accomplishment, of the money, or of the success. Self-sabotage happens all the time.

In some circles you will hear this also referred to as your lizard brain. The term "lizard brain" is a light-hearted way of describing the most primitive part of our human brain. The human version of the lizard brain has been evolving for around 285 million years, and is similar in power and concept to the total brain capacity of a modern lizard, thus the phrase "lizard brain". There is a more in-depth explanation in Mr. Godin's *Linchpin:*

> *The lizard brain is hungry, scared, angry, and horny. The lizard brain only wants to eat and be safe. The lizard brain will fight (to the death) if it has to, but would rather run away. It likes a vendetta and has no trouble getting angry. The lizard brain cares what everyone else thinks, because status in the tribe is essential to its survival. The lizard brain is the reason you're afraid, the reason you do not do all the art you can, the reason you do not ship when you can. The lizard brain is the source of the resistance.*

Our lizard brain is what sabotages ourselves more often than not. The lizard brain wants conformity and is happy with conformity. We all have a lizard brain.

The good news, however, is all of these erroneous paradigms can be reprogrammed. All of your beliefs can be changed and your lizard brain can be, to a certain extent, controlled. You have the ability to program what it is you want to now believe, what you now want to accomplish, and what you now want to be. To begin that exercise you first have to get very, very clear on what it is you want and what you want the rest of your life to look like. Clearly identify what your purpose is here and what you want the dash between your birth and your leaving this earth says to others. What do you want to accomplish through determination, hard work, and tenacity? What results do you want from those efforts?

Write those things down. Develop your perfect week or month in a few sentences, and write them out to read to yourself over and over again. Put together a vision board of your life, the way you project it; visualize it, and see it every day. As the old saying goes, "A picture is worth a thousand words." Our brains works in pictures so we should give them the pictures they can work with. Be thankful for what it is you already have and write down all the things you are grateful for today. Write out a few affirmations affirming your beliefs. I have eight affirmations that I have been reading out loud to myself and have deeply believed in for over 15 years. All of my success in life and business I attribute to believing in it, visualizing it, affirming it, and achieving it.

It is absolutely amazing when it all comes together. Earl Nightingale once said in his famous presentation *The Strangest Secret*: "You become what you think about." So you better be very clear about what you are thinking about!

Here are what a few things others have said about our minds, and how we think, throughout history:

- Marcos Aurelius, the great Roman emperor said, "A man's life is what his thoughts make of it."
- Ralph Waldo Emerson said, "Man is what he thinks about all day long."
- William James said, "The greatest discovery of my generation is that human beings can alter their lives by altering their attitudes of mind."
- In the Bible, Mark 9:23: "If thou canst believe, all things are possible to him that believeth."
- Dr. Norman Vincent Peale said, "Believe and succeed."
- William Shakespeare said, "Our doubts are traitors, and make us lose the good we might oft win, by fearing to attempt."
- And this from George Bernard Shaw, "People are always blaming their circumstances for what they are. I do not believe in circumstances. The people who get on in this world are the people who get up and look for the circumstances they want, and if they can't find them, make them."

Your life today can be completely different in a year or two from today, and it is all in your control. The question becomes: Do you want to change your life? Do you have a reason, a *why*, a Personal Mission Statement that is not your reality today?

If you do, then the only thing holding you back from a new reality, and living your Personal Mission, is getting clear on your thoughts, on what you want, on who you can help, on changing your beliefs, and on living your Personal Mission Statement.

To do so, you will need to make the commitment to engage in personal development. Take an hour a day, call it your "power hour" to get clear on your purpose, your mission, visualize what you want, control your thoughts, and move into action to create the life you want.

A Few Ways to Create the Life You Want

- *Decide what you want:* Interestingly enough, we sometimes go through life without ever really thinking about what it is we want out of life. What do you want? Decide what your purpose is, develop a Personal Mission Statement to live your life by. If you live your purpose and your mission, everything else will fall into place (To design a mission statement, Go to www.franklincovey.com/msb/)
- *Get quiet:* Our world is very noisy and very busy these days. We sometimes do not take the time to just get quiet, to think about what we are grateful for—you may want to consider a gratitude journal—to appreciate where you are, and what you have in your life. For a little perspective, Jim Rohn once said, "America is easy. Bangladesh and India are hard." Get quiet, take some time to meditate, or pray, have clarity of outcome, vision yourself with exactly what you want; emotionally-laden, sensory rich visions of your outcome.
- *Get some help by reading or listening:* Take 15 minutes of your "Power Hour" each day to read a chapter of a book, or listen to an audio CD of an inspiring piece that fits with your purpose. Here are a few of my favorites:
    - *The Four Agreements* by Don Miguel Ruiz
    - *The Game of Life and How to Play It* by Florence Scovel Shinn
    - *Start With Why* by Simon Sinek
    - *The Attractor Factor* by Dr. Joe Vitale
    - *Think and Grow Rich* by Napoleon Hill
    - *The Strangest Secret* by Earl Nightingale
    - *The Success Principles* by Jack Canfield
- *Make a vision board:* Visioning exactly want you want is as important as thinking about it. See what you want, get what you see. Albert Einstein once said, "Imagination is everything. It is the preview of life's coming attractions." A vision board is simply your desire in pictures. Put them on a board, and fill it up with your dreams! And then each day, during your power hour, look

at the board, visualize everything on it as if you have already accomplished it! That is the key.

- *Join or start a mastermind group:* Sharing and learning from like-minded individuals is a powerful way to begin changing your paradigm. There are many groups already established with the goal of personal development. If you cannot find one, start one yourself! It just takes an hour or an hour and a half a week and can be very effective.
- *Exercise:* Without your health, nothing else really matters. Your body is your temple and should be treated that way. Get some exercise each week. It does not even need to be much; a walk will do it, three times a week. When exercising, it is also a great time to listen to an inspirational message on an iPod or phone.
- *Drink plenty of water:* Ninety percent of the human body is water. All of our organs and systems work with water. All of the toxins we eat and breathe are eliminated by the body through water. Other than oxygen, there is nothing more important than water. Yet, we sometimes take water for granted and do not take in each day what our body desires. Sometimes feeling hungry is not hunger at all, but a need for water. Try it. Drink at least a gallon of water a day!
- *Turn off the negative:* Turning off the negative is simply turning off the news. Try this: for the next 30 days, do not watch any news, read any newspaper, or go to any news sites on the Internet; just be in the moment, think about your Personal Mission, take action on your business, and see how you feel after 30 days.
- *Take action:* It will take doing all of the above with determination and action to accomplish your goals in life. Many of the seminar and workshop gurus will talk about all the things that are very important within one's self, such as the Law of Attraction, but they sometimes miss the most important factor of all. Without any action, without determination and some tenacity, without a work ethic, without getting out there and learning, seeking, building relationships, or contributing, nothing will matter.
- *Reevaluate and plan-do-review:* Finally, constantly make sure you are on course, and course correct if needed. Each month, reevaluate your month and audit yourself. Did you accomplish what you

had intended? Did you get a bit closer to your goals? Did you take the action necessary to move the ball down the court? It is the self-evaluation, the self-assessment that will help you stay the course or course adjust if something is just not working.

If you are clear, have your *why* established and your personal mission statement, are working on the brand YOU first, and taking action, then everything else will fall into place with the "Perfect Business, Inc.," for you.

Chapter 5

Mining Your Passion

"Choose a job you love,
and you will never have to work a day in your life."

– Confucius

Working hard for something we do not care about is called stress; working hard for something we love is called passion.

Passion, from the Latin verb *patī* meaning to suffer, is a term applied to a very strong feeling about a person or thing. Passion is an intense emotion compelling feeling, enthusiasm, or desire for something.

The term is also often applied to a lively or eager interest in or admiration for a proposal, cause, or activity or love; to a feeling of unusual excitement, enthusiasm or compelling emotion; a positive affinity or love, towards a subject.

There are different reasons individuals are motivated for a profession. One of these includes passion for the profession. When an individual is passionate about their profession they tend to be less obsessive about their behavior while on their job, resulting in more work being done and more work satisfaction. These same individuals have higher levels of psychological well-being. When people genuinely enjoy their profession and are motivated by their passion, they tend to be more satisfied with their work and more psychologically healthy. When an individual is unsatisfied with their profession they are also dissatisfied with their family relationships and experience psychological distress.

Other reasons people are more satisfied when they are motivated by their passion for their profession include the effects of intrinsic and external motivations. When an individual is doing the job to satisfy others, they tend have lower levels of satisfaction and psychological health. These same individuals have shown they are motivated by several beliefs and fears concerning other people. Next, though some individuals believe one should not work extreme hours, many prefer it because of how passionate they are about what they do. On the other hand, this may also put a strain on family relationships and friendships. The balance of the two is something that is hard to achieve, and it is always hard to satisfy both parties. This is why working for someone else, building someone else's dream (think Corporate America) usually does not elicit passion from its employees. Being an employee can, and does, pay the bills, but it rarely brings out true passion in a person.

Many times when I have asked employees of various companies I was consulting for if they liked their job, if they felt fulfilled, if they enjoyed coming to work every day, I would get an answer like, "Well, yes, it is a good job," or "It has its benefits." But rarely, very rarely, would I hear a passionate answer to the *why* of what they were doing for a living. It is the difference between earning a living and living a great life. And it is most likely the reason why nearly 80 percent of working people interviewed recently said that they really did not like their job. It is just that: a job. It is hard to get pumped up when the feeling is "it is just a job, something I must do because everyone else does it." There is that conformity thing again!

Passion, however, is the energy that comes from bringing more of YOU into what you do.

Simply put, it is being who you are and doing what comes naturally. When what you do is in alignment with who you are, you get energy from doing it. It is like water flowing along its natural riverbed. It actually gains energy from the path it is taking; compare that to what most people experience in their work, which is more like trying to force it up and over a mountain.

How do you consciously, consistently bring more of you into what you do?

One simple approach is to go beyond what you love and ask why you love it. Do some reverse engineering to identify the underlying characteristics that tend to be in place when you are on fire. Gathering the resulting insights in one place gives you a passion-focused decision tool. Think of it as an internal compass that takes the heart-based passion decision and puts it in the realm that the analytical mind can understand as well.

It takes the guesswork out of the process and lets you make a more concrete evaluation. For example, you can look at a potential business or job and ask, "How well does this align with these underlying characteristics?" You can do the same with any choice you make. Simply ask the question, "Will this bring me closer to alignment with what energizes me, or farther away?"

The better you get at identifying exactly what it is that drives you, what makes you happy, what you would do if money was not a concern, and what you want the rest of your life to look like, the easier it will be to live on purpose. The better you get at understanding you first, the easier it will be to find exactly what it is you should do, to answer the question, "Okay, so what now?"

Then, stay focused, take action and never, ever, ever, give up! I have been amazed over the years at the number of individuals who get started with something, anything, and then, right before they are to reap the rewards of their hard work, they give up. Many times it is because they just never realize how close they really are to success. Many times, because of the instant gratification society we now live in, they do not understand the law of compounding, leveraging, or any of the other principles in this book. It is just such a shame when someone with a purpose, a passion, a why, starts and, before they finish the task or job, they quit. They lose faith in themselves, lose their passion for what it is they wanted, lose the dream, and go back into the cow pasture of life. If you find it, do not give up until you have accomplished your why, your dream!

Someone once sent me an email about those who had a passion, and stayed the course, never gave up, until they reached the destination they were dreaming about. Many of these people you know—they are in our history books—but did you ever know how easy it could have been for any one of them to quit?

Here are some examples of notable historical figures that never gave up:

- As a young man, Abraham Lincoln went to war as a captain and returned as a private. Afterwards, he was a failure as a businessman. As a lawyer in Springfield, he was too impractical and temperamental to be a success. He turned to politics and was defeated in his first try for the legislature, defeated in his first attempt to be nominated for Congress, then defeated in his application to be commissioner of the General Land Office, defeated in the Senatorial election of 1854, defeated again in his efforts for the vice-presidency in 1856, and, finally, defeated in the senatorial election of 1858. He later became the 16th President of the United States of America.

- Winston Churchill failed sixth grade. He was also defeated in every election for public office until he became Prime Minister at the age of 62. He wrote, "Never give in, never give in, never, never, never, never—in nothing, great or small, large or petty—never give in except to convictions of honor and good sense. Never, never, never, never give up."
- Thomas Edison's teachers said he was "too stupid to learn anything." He was fired from his first two jobs for being "non-productive." As an inventor, Edison made 1,000 unsuccessful attempts at inventing the light bulb. When a reporter asked, "How did it feel to fail 1,000 times?" Edison replied, "I didn't fail 1,000 times. The light bulb was an invention with 1,000 steps."
- Albert Einstein did not speak until he was four years old and did not read until he was seven. His parents thought he was "sub-normal," and one of his teachers described him as "mentally slow, unsociable, and adrift forever in foolish dreams." He was expelled from school and was refused admittance to the Zurich Polytechnic School. He did eventually learn to speak and read. Even to do a little math.
- Henry Ford failed and went broke five times before he succeeded.
- R. H. Macy failed seven times before his store in New York City caught on.
- F. W. Woolworth was not allowed to wait on customers when he worked in a dry goods store because, his boss said, "he didn't have enough sense."

- An expert said of Vince Lombardi: "He possesses minimal football knowledge and lacks motivation." Lombardi would later write, "It is not whether you get knocked down; it is whether you get back up."
- Babe Ruth is famous for his home run record, but for decades he also held the record for strikeouts. He hit 714 home runs and struck out 1,330 times in his career, about which he said, "Every strike brings me closer to the next home run."
- Tom Landry, Chuck Noll, Bill Walsh, and Jimmy Johnson accounted for 11 of the 19 Super Bowl victories from 1974 to 1993. They also share the distinction of having the worst records of first-season head coaches in NFL history—they did not win a single game.
- Have you ever heard the Mark Victor Hansen and Jack Canfield story of the *Chicken Soup for the Soul* book? They just knew it was a hit, but were rejected over and over and over again by all the major publishing houses. Ultimately, that book, and all the other books in the *Chicken Soup for the Soul* series, are the second bestselling book series of all time, behind the Bible.
- We will end with Woody Allen: "I do not want to achieve immortality through my work. I want to achieve it through not dying. Eighty percent of success is showing up."

Do not ever give up, as long as you are emotionally vested, that is. Do not let others stop you from achieving success in life. There are all kinds of people who will pop up in your life, who are not really excited for your potential success because they do not want you to pass them up psychologically. In a CD series I once listened to by master entrepreneurial trainer Jerry Clark, he called it the Murphy's Committee, and the committee is everywhere. This committee is made up of your family, peers, friends, and neighbors who are all just looking out for you. They will tell you things like "You do not really think you can do that, do you?" or "Really, you are going to try to do that?" and "Oh, my cousin's boyfriend's mother tried something like that and it just does not work." If you try to get out of the box, out of the comfort zone of conformity, you will hear all kinds of comments. The absolute best advice though, is to find your passion, your energy, your purpose, and your dreams, set out on a path to achieve them, go at it as if failure is not an option, do not listen to the naysayers and never, ever, ever, ever, give up! Yes, you can!

So, have you downloaded the 27 questions to find your passion workbook at www.liveyourlegend.net yet?

Chapter 6

Perfect Business, Inc.

"Money never made anyone rich."

– Seneca

There is a blueprint, a map, and a plan for the perfect business. It does not really matter what the product is in this business; it can be anything from an Internet downloadable manual or book to home emergency generators to vitamins. This perfect business is what your search must be in order to fully secure your future. The Perfect Business, Inc. is all about you: it is taking into consideration your vision, why, and passion; adding in some purpose and goal of leaving a legacy, and then mixing it all together with latest trends, advancing technologies, and generational understanding. It is all about 'you' being the economy, not at all about 'the stated economy'. I found it very interesting with the latest recession how so many people were affected, but I was not, because I am my own economy. You can be too with the Perfect Business, Inc. Answering the question, "What would I be doing everyday if money was no object?" should help you get to the correct answer for you, the Perfect Business, Inc.

Every day, more businesses fail than succeed. Your odds of picking a potential failure are rather high if you do not put in the work ahead of time. Business is changing dramatically due to the evolution of marketing methods, specifically lowering the cost of presentation. The goal must be to cut through all the noise and have something of value to offer. Even a decade ago, the cost of printing, typesetting, mailing, and communications made business start-ups impossible for most people. Now, with the refinement of the Internet, it is possible for a high school student to reach out to a thousand or more people with one minute of effort on a handheld smartphone. Search engine optimization

(SEO) a decade ago was a six figure expense; today the same or superior results can be obtained for a few thousand dollars or less.

A quality e-commerce website a decade ago could easily cost one hundred thousand dollars. Today, high school students can build one in a few days for allowance money. I recently hired a high schooler to build me a new fantastic website, and I hired male and female voice-over artists for a great price at www.fiverr.com. I can get anything done now at almost the speed of light; it is amazing! Things have changed, and marketing, more than any time in our history, can be made to look fantastic. The overwhelming amount of information we now receive every single day can be numbing. With the Connection Economy, it will be more about building trust, along with the law of consumerism we will be detailing later. But because of all the noise, the cluttering of the marketplace, because everything is so fast, you have to work harder than ever to get your message out. You simply must not take no for an answer, until the no means, "I understand what I am saying no to."

No does not mean no in effectively building an enterprise. In today's sophisticated business world, the buyer is not just better informed, they are 'Google informed'. No must mean *not right now* and must be anticipated in advance of making any kind of sales presentation, or starting any kind of business. In my professional business life experience, I have always steered people to only considering the Perfect Business, Inc. for their personal and professional self, doing life on purpose, not by accident.

To find the Perfect Business, Inc. one has to first establish a powerful motivation to learn the facts of what makes up the perfect system, and then jump into the business with serious intent, committed effort, and determination. In order to do that you must establish a powerful belief. As discussed previously, the word 'belief' is so important; it truly is one of the most important words in the human language.

Believe it, you will achieve it, but doubt it, you will probably live without it.

I call your belief your unconscious intuition. It is a combination of your beliefs, your convictions, and your mindset that will allow you to reach your why with resolve. Only when you change your beliefs, will you change your actions, which in turn will change your results; you will achieve the results you really want. Failure cannot be an option.

The Perfect Business, Inc. must take into consideration all trends, both demographic and generational, and must be able to look ahead at trends. An analogy would be what the great hockey star, Wayne Gretzky, once said: "I skate to where the puck is going, not to where it has been." Go to where the puck is going, and you will increase your chances for the Perfect Business, Inc.

As an example, recent statistics have a huge Baby Boomer bubble coming—well, continuing would be a better term—with the age group of those between 60–70 years old doubling over the next 10 years! There are around 80 million Boomers in the U.S. and Canada. That is a huge portion of the population entering a completely different segment of their adult lives. I know this to be true as I am one of those Boomers, right smack in the middle of this phenomenon. There are some really important things to understand about this group as it relates to buying habits and what they will be looking for, as well as their income habits and how well they manage into the senior years.

If you look at all the upcoming trends, the Wellness Revolution is just one that will grow at unprecedented rates over the next one or two decades. These aging Boomers are going to spend an enormous amount of money to stay ahead of time. There are a couple of well-known statistics about this group as it relates to being overweight or obese, about the advent of diabetes and other catastrophic health concerns, and about the health care costs associated with poor health. It has been stated that $1 spent on Wellness yields a savings of $3 in reactive health care costs later. This is a huge insight into heading to where the puck is going. The old saying that an ounce of prevention is worth a pound of cure is coming true in a big, big way. And the Perfect Business Inc. could possibly be one that takes this trend into consideration, if you have a passion for health and wellness.

Furthermore, this Boomer generation, especially the ones in the 55–65 year old segment, are finding that they did not do a very good job saving for senior living. Fidelity Investment research recently found that the average boomer couple will need approximately $4,800 a month to live a standard lifestyle. Social Security may fund about half of that amount, maybe, and only 40 percent of this population has the capability to have the other half available which, again, gives a huge insight into how you can position Perfect Business, Inc. in a way to benefit for years to come. Can you find a solution for you that includes giving this segment an opportunity too? That is a big win.

There is another trend just as strong and just as important coming down the pike. It has to do with the Gen-Y generation. This generation is sometimes called the Millennials or the Echo Boomers, but it is another huge group of potential consumers going through a new part of their lives, around 77 million of them! The members of Gen-Y have been deeply affected by the events of the past few decades and have become so tech dependent that a whole new set of circumstances exist if you are going to attract the Gen-Ys. They have practiced what is called "delayed adulthood," mostly due to their Boomer parents, and they are just now entering the phase of life where they will become a huge segment of the buying public.

Some of the interesting trends coming out of this generation, as identified by Jason Dorsey at the Center for Generational Kinetics, is that the Gen-Ys have the least established loyalty to brand name and brand products, have little to no negative perception to direct sales, network marketing, or other new economy ways; and are most likely to refer business to you if they like what you are offering. Here is another big trend clue for you; it has been stated that Gen-Y will outspend the Baby Boomers by 2017. This is just another example of studying trends.

There are trends other than generational to be aware of as well, like the trend that is saying that transactional income is not keeping up with inflation. If you look closely at the last 10 years or so, you will see that the average wages in the U.S. have been flat to down, while the average cost of basically everything has continued to rise. We discussed the reasons around this earlier: it is the new way of paying on performance and what the market will bear. In 2013 we began to see, for the first time, non-union workers striking at fast food restaurants all over the country and at various Wal*Marts throughout. The net effect of all of this is a reduction in the standard of living that people have become accustomed to. It is why over 70 percent of wage earning Americans now say that they are basically living paycheck to paycheck; the paycheck is just paying the monthly cost of living, with little to none left over for savings or discretionary spending. More and more folks are in the 'living wage' segment of society today. Do you really want to start a business in today's world that relies upon discretionary dollars?

And what about the idea that we should 'Buy U.S.'? This is not even a trend, but a movement, and movements can be much more powerful than trends. This non-partisan, non-political movement is about folks finally realizing that this "race to the bottom," as I call it, has not fared well for our economy. The movement of jobs outside the U.S., the movement of manufacturing and the movement of money, all outside the borders of the U.S. and Canada, have taken not only the actual jobs but also many ancillary jobs, too. It is actually worse than what the average person even realizes. Not only is the bankruptcy of a major industrial city like Detroit a clue, but if you look up the Wall Street Journal article from May 10, 2012, the headline says it all about the 'old' use-to-be-American company, Proctor & Gamble: "Goodbye Cincinnati, Hello Singapore." The article was about the company's move of their Consumer Products Division out of the United States. So not only has Proctor & Gamble moved most, if not all, of its manufacturing outside the country, but is even now moving its Division Headquarters away. It is this race to the bottom that has some grassroots movement starting, really just beginning, like the Million Jobs Project (www.millionjobsproject.us) and American Made Matters, (www.americanmadematters.com). How can you become part of the solution?

Perfect Business, Inc must not only take into account belief, passion, purpose, and determination, but also some knowledge of trends, going to where the puck is heading.

So here is a question for you: do you truly believe with all your heart that the business you are thinking about starting, or currently doing, will take you where you want to go? Is it the right time—an upcoming trend—and are you at the right place? Will it bless the lives of the people you will be soliciting to? With all of your soul, do you feel it is amazing and life changing? Are you thinking, doing, and planning from your heart or from your head?

There is a new normal out there, and the Perfect Business, Inc. must take into account this new normal for you to be successful: doing it on purpose.

These are the really important questions to answer; not just what the commission is, what the spreads are, and what the bottom line is to get going. If you truly believe you are invincible with your Perfect Business Inc. business, you are building a business with heart. You have what others are looking for. You understand the emotional attachment someone will make with the *why*.

With the Perfect Business, Inc., you must also understand the Law of Diffusion of Innovation:

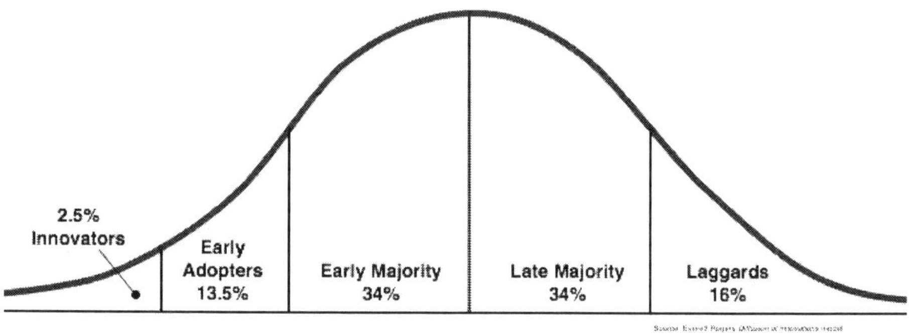

Our population is broken into five segments that fall across a bell shape curve. These five segments are identified as the innovators, the early adopters, the early majority, late majority and the laggards. Around 50 percent of the population are the late majority, and the laggards. In fact, the 16 percent or so of the laggards will never buy anything from you, your store, etc. just because. If you have something of great benefit, something that will change the world for the better, 50 percent of the population will be late to the party, with a portion never getting into the party. As Jim Rohn said, "It is just the way it is, and if you want to change it, well, you will have to wait until you get your own planet!"

So, not everyone you talk to about your business will be interested; in fact, many will not want to even give you the time of day. There is a very good reason for this, as explained by Simon Sinek in *Start with Why*. According to Mr. Sinek, "The goal is not to do business with everyone who needs what you have. The goal is to do business with those who believe what you believe." You see, if someone does not believe that they need what you are offering, if it does not fit that person's personal mission, vision, or needs, then they will not partake, even though you may know in your heart that everyone needs what you have. The people who become your champions, your evangelists, in any business, product or service, are those who believe the way you do. It is the same if you have employees. Your best employees will be those who believe in what you are doing, how you are making the world a better place.

This is why when you get a "no," you must really work it to make sure they know exactly what they are saying no to, since many times, they will say no, due to lack of information or understanding. I see this every day in my business. I am extremely passionate about my business and I believe that it is the absolute best business and Business Model that I have ever seen—total belief. I have seen lives change over and over again. Each night, before bed, I can look in the mirror and be proud and happy at the face looking back at me. I am leaving a legacy for my children and others. Yet, every week, I speak to folks who do not see what I see, who do not believe, who have become hardened, probably a bit cynical, and resigned with their fate in life. The old saying of not seeing the forest for the trees applies here. It is just the way it is, and there is nothing you can do to change it, so do not try! Find those who believe the same way you do.

The Perfect Business, Inc. is all about you, all about how well prepared you are, how well informed on near future trends and happenings, how much you have coming from your heart, not your head. Perfect Business Inc. is out there; I found it, and I know you can too.

Chapter 7

Understanding Transactional Income vs Residual Income (Leverage)

"Much of what we see depends on what we are looking for."

– Phil Calloway

In my humble opinion, this is one of the most important discussions we will have in this book: understanding the differences between transactional income and residual income, then applying what you learn. Pay close attention here, understanding exactly what it takes to create a residual-style income will set you free. Residual income will allow you to meet all your dreams, have the time freedom to be purposeful, to give back, and to leave a legacy for others. It was one of the most important discoveries of my life, second only to the fact that we become what we think about.

The word "transaction" has numerous applications in both business law and business execution. I will simplify our application to make this very understandable. First, take the word at its basic definition, to transact or exchange something. If I have an agreement to work for you for an hour and I charge $25.00 for my one hour of work, then we have a business transaction. I am exchanging one hour of my life for $25.00 and you are giving up $25.00 of cash for that exchange of my time and effort. A transaction.

To get to the specific point that I want to make, we will define our application of transaction income. Transactional income includes amounts of cash exchanged for goods or services. For example, any business that sets up operations and hires employees, then uses their labor to provide services to its customers is earning transaction revenue. That business is exchanging those services for cash and cash equivalents. Likewise the businesses that sell the original business the supplies needed to set up their operations and the employees hired by them are also earning transaction income because they are exchanging products or services for their cash earnings.

In case there is still some confusion, we will reverse the definition. Non-transaction revenue is revenue received without the business or individual performing an immediate exchange of equal or near-equal value. An example of non-transaction income is taxes. Another example would be royalties from a book or investment.

One of the most important principles of this book is understanding the real difference between creating a consistent transactional income stream, and a consistent residual income stream. Most of us, as we are starting our careers in the workforce after schooling, start in transactional income. We really do not even give it a thought. That is the way it has always been, that is the way my parents earned an income, that is the way of the land, that is how the Industrial economy works; we conform. So we travel down the road of transactional income but without ever really understanding why we seem to never get ahead. Why there seems to be so much month left at the end of the money. There are a couple ways to evaluate whether you have transactional income vs. true residual income.

I first discovered this phenomenon, which was always right in front of me, by reading Robert Kiyosaki's *Cash Flow Quadrant*, his sequel to *Rich Dad Poor Dad*. Here it is:

Transactional Income

The left side of the Quadrant below, the E and S side, is where transactional income occurs. It is also where around 98 percent of all jobs and businesses occur. It is either being an employee, earning an hourly wage or salary, or being self-employed, like a doctor, dentist, realtor, chiropractor, landscaper, small restaurant owner, individual franchise owner, etc. You "own" a job.

We trade time for money, or if we are in sales we are paid every time we sell a product or service. What would happen if the job or career was

Robert Kiyosaki's CASHFLOW Quadrant

no longer required? What would happen if the economy caused a significant slowdown in your sales? Then this type of income goes away. Time for money, time for service, time for a sale. It really does not matter how educated you are, how valuable your service might be, or how large the sale is. Transaction income is one-time income and it can go away or be reduced very, very quickly.

Do you work a job currently where someone else pays you an hourly wage or a salary? If so, that is a great indication that you have transactional income in the E Quadrant. Can you ever take some time off, say, three months, and still be paid? The answer is a resounding no. If you do not show up, you make no money; it is trading time for money. I know that most of us, me included, looked forward to achieving five years on our job so we could receive two weeks of paid vacation. Then wow, when we made the 10 year mark we got four weeks of paid vacation. Woohoo! That made our year!

I have so many friends that sit around talking about how many weeks they have this year and what they plan to do with their couple of weeks of freedom. Many years ago I started thinking about how silly that is and how we cherish a few weeks off the job each year. We do it because that is the way it has always been for most of us. Working a job with transactional income will most certainly pay the monthly bills, but will it let you really live a more purposeful, passionate life, with some real freedom and a long term plan? Not really. Will it allow you to leave a legacy? Doubtful.

Transactional income is not just about a job and working for someone with an hourly or salary wage. It is also about those who are self-employed, the largest makeup of workers in the world, the S Quadrant. Self-employed are those individuals with their own small business: doctors, dentists, chiropractors, realtors, loan processors, lawyers, CPAs, landscapers, consultants, drycleaner owners, many franchisee owners, etc., Look at the facts: A recent study by the U.S. Small Business Administration's (SBA) Office of Advocacy counted 26.8 million businesses in the United States. Of those, 99 percent have fewer than 500 employees and as such are considered small businesses. This means that only one percent have more than 500 employees. Yet, more notable is the fact that according to the U.S. Census Bureau, 98.2 percent have fewer than 100 employees. If you are impressed with that number, you may be amazed to learn that in the same report it states that 89.3 percent of the businesses in America have fewer than 20 employees!

Bear with me for just a moment more as I drive this point home. Even more amazing is the fact that 78.6 percent have fewer than 10 employees and 60.8 percent have fewer than five employees.

Here is the point. Sixty percent to 80 percent of all small businesses in the U.S. have no leverage; they are again stuck in transactional income. It is unlikely that the owners of a small business can leave their place of work for, say, six months, go on an around the world cruise, and come back to a viable running business. Many of the small business owners out there are actually chained to their business, not able to get away from it because they *are* the business. I recently had an experience with my drycleaner that really brought this point home for me more than ever.

Visiting my drycleaner one day recently, there was a sign on the door which read "We will be closed from September 3–10th and will open again on September 11th." Now I have been going to the same drycleaner every week for 18 years, and this was the very first time that they closed for a vacation! I said to the owners, "Holy smokes, you guys are actually getting away, going on a vacation?" And the owner said "Yes, can you believe it? I wouldn't close the business for the week but I do not have anyone else that can run the store while we are gone, so we will close." After 18 years, they are taking a week off.

That my friends, is transactional, chained-to-your business income. You are the business and it is hard to get away from it! It is all transactional, and it provides for a living, without any freedom to really live a more purposeful or passionate life. Transactional income is a way of life. It works for many, does not work for others. And I am certainly not saying that you cannot make enough income in the E or S Quadrant to get to the eventual 'win', the 'I' Quadrant, but what was pointed out to me in *Cash Flow Quadrant* was that taxes and other liabilities will keep us less than whole within the E and S Quadrants. It is also the main cog of the Industrial Economy, which is now passing. In the new normal, the Connection Economy, there is currently a blur between transactional and the residual-style income we will discuss next. So just make sure to understand the differences here before making a decision about your next step.

One last thought on transaction income. The slaves that built Egypt's pyramids were actually, for the most part, not slaves, but employees. They were paid or given housing, food, and if they were sick or injured, doctors would care for them. They were in different skill levels, and had different levels of status and pay for what they did. There were common laborers and skilled craftsman, architects and carpenters, engineers and food handlers, all working on the pharaoh's construction project.

Tell me, how different are we today? Is transactional income slavery? I find the line between slavery and job to be a very wispy division, at best.

Residual Income

Actors have it: every time *Titanic* is sold or played, Leo and Kate earn residuals. Songwriters have it: Paul McCartney has enjoyed decades of earnings from songs he wrote "Yesterday." Inventors have it: Bill Gates has carved out a reasonable living from income received every time his software is used.

Do you have it? When you look at the possibility of true residual income, it is an idea, which everyone should want, few have, and ever fewer even think about.

Famous billionaire J Paul Getty once said, "I would rather earn 1 percent off 100 people's efforts than 100 percent off of mine"; that, my friends, is all about residual income. How would you like to do the work one time, say 10 years earlier, yet get paid every time the work is being viewed, purchased, or used? The only financial blessing in the business universe that is more desirable than pure residual income, is viral-residual income.

The word viral sprang up with the Internet, because it is exactly that: information that is started by you and carried without your permission or control to thousands or millions of other people. Like catching a cold or a flu, a virus can be transmitted by a handshake, and then it is out of your control, having changed hands and bodies thousands of times having long forgotten it passed through you.

Likewise, a business sent out on the Internet is almost instantly capable of sailing virally to endless corners of the known world, with or without your help or permission. This new Connection Economy is changing the way people look at the traditional ways. If you can find a solution with a viral way to spread, along with a consistent way to monetize (think subscription), then you have the possibility of a true residual income stream.

Let me make something clear, however, about residual income. Sometimes we see residual income called passive income. I have a hard time buying the term passive income, though. I just have never seen someone create a residual income stream, call it passive, and for it to continue as is for the rest of life. It usually takes ongoing work and ongoing effort, to have a true, ongoing, lifelong residual income stream. I do not see anything passive about it. It takes work at the beginning, middle and end. If not, the income usually goes down, eventually to nothing. The old saying that there is no free lunch is true; everything in life takes work unless you are one of the few trust fund babies, won millions in the lottery, or had some huge inheritance that already has money making money (the 'I' Quadrant at work).

Passive income comes more from the I Quadrant, investing your money to make money. However, in order to reach the I Quadrant, you need money that will be put to work to make money, and that is where the transactional or residual income streams come into play. It is difficult with transactional income to make it to the I Quadrant since your bills, taxes, and other liabilities usually leave little to invest, and the residual income stream takes time, patience, and work. Residual income is not passive income; there is a difference here.

Residual income can come in various forms too. We already mentioned that actors, musicians, and authors have some residual income. It is income, however, which for actors, musicians, and authors decreases over time, sometimes down to nothing, because the instrument that created it, such as movie, book, music, decreases in desire—and sales—over time. An author continues to write books because the initial thrust of book sales lasts a while, but then dwindles as the folks who want to buy that particular book begin to dissipate. Same goes for movies and music. A friend of mine is a stunt actor for Westerns. He lives in Tucson, Arizona and is close to the filming locations for Westerns: Old Tucson Studios and Tombstone. As a stunt actor, he has been in numerous westerns, some very recognizable ones. I was at his home one day about a year ago when he opened a piece of mail from Paramount Studios with a check enclosed. It was for a movie he did in the 90s and the residual check was for five cents. Yes, five cents! We both got a real laugh out of his movie acting career and the ongoing residual income he had!

Another story of residual income is one of my favorites: it is the story of Myron Cope's Terrible Towel. The Terrible Towel is a rally towel associated with the Pittsburgh Steelers, an American football team in the National Football League (NFL). Created in 1975 by then-Steelers radio broadcaster Myron Cope, the Terrible Towel has spread in popularity. Fans take their Towel to famous sites while on vacation. The Towel has been taken to the peak of Mount Everest and even into space on the International Space Station. It is widely recognized as a symbol of the Steelers and the city of Pittsburgh.

In 1996, Cope gave the rights to the Terrible Towel to the Allegheny Valley School in Coraopolis, Pennsylvania. The school provides care for more than 900 people with mental and physical disabilities, including Cope's autistic son, Danny. Proceeds from the Terrible Towel have helped raise more than $2.2 million for the school. During the 2008 season, when the Steelers won their sixth Super Bowl, more than 1 million Towels were sold; some fans bought 200 Towels at a time. Now that is true residual income, and it is all going to a great cause. Mr. Cope had a purpose, a passion, and left a legacy that keeps on going, long after his death. So you can certainly create a residual income stream by inventing something which catches on and becomes a mainstay of society.

Then there is a story that really got me thinking, many years ago, about the power of residual income. In 1985, while climbing the corporate ladder at Circle K, I was introduced to an individual whose family was the number one distributor with a Canadian Network

Marketing company. As I got to know this young man, and his family, I began to understand the great things that one can accomplish with a life of residual income. They were very, very successful, and I even remember once being shown their combined family income for one month: it was around $380,000. That kind of monthly income can do a lot of great things for others. I could not get that out of my mind after that experience in the early 90s: the kind of impact one could have with their life by earning a no-ceiling kind of residual income stream. What a dream. Unfortunately, for that family, the business did not last. Major flaws in the MLM compensation structure and ownership caused the company to crash, and along with it, the residual income that this family had built. So, even though residual income is a wonderful way to build something that should last a lifetime, it is really more about finding the right company that you are passionate about, with the right Business Model that will outlast your lifetime.

Residual income is the kind of ongoing, consistent income with which one could make a difference in the world. The only catch: how do you find it, how do you analyze its staying power, where is it, and how do you receive it?

We will see if we can give you some tools to be able to figure out the answers to those questions.

Chapter 8

So You Have A Business Idea?

"It is the constant and determined effort that breaks down all resistance, sweeps away all obstacles."

- Claude M. Bristol

I have been fortunate through my working life to have been involved in and around numerous Business Models. That worldwide experience has given me a unique perspective on why, when you are deciding "what is next in my life," that you select a business idea and model that you understand, is a leading trend model, and you have passion for. Probably the most important ingredient is always going to be your passion. But even passion cannot withstand a poorly designed Business Model and concept with poor delivery to the marketplace. Everything we do as a business always includes some sort of delivery of goods or services to the masses via some sort of consumption; or business-to-business with the same purpose, a delivery of goods or services to the marketplace. Let us take a look at the Top 25 companies on the 2013 Fortune 500 listing of the top publicly-traded companies:

Company	Revenue ($ Billions)
Wal*Mart	469.2
Exxon-Mobil	449.9
Chevron	233.9

Phillips 66	169.6
Bank of America Corp.	100.1
Costco Wholesale	99.1
Kroger	96.8
Express Scripts Holding	94.4
Wells Fargo	91.2

Seventeen of the top 25 companies in the world are involved in consumerism as it relates to goods and services we need and use, many times, daily, weekly and monthly. When you add in the consumption of health care and financial products, then it covers all 25. It is an extremely important fact to understand when searching for your next move that if it includes some product or service that is consistently consumed, and repurchased, then you have a chance for an ongoing sustainable business. But that product or service has to fit the law of consumerism.

The law of consumerism is not a law that you will find in a dictionary or encyclopedia. It is a law that I define as consumption occurs; in trust, need, convenience, and price. As you see above, the Fortune 500 largest companies are all about consumption. I always say that consumption is a gold mine. It is what we do all of our life. If you really look at consumerism however, you will see that it is really a very modern way of life. Think about it. When the Baby Boomers were growing up, which was just in the last 50 or 60 years, there were one-car families, if they had a car; the television was just being developed, so, everyone had a little black and white TV; maybe a radio or phonograph in the living room; and the basics to live on. Then, if you were born before 1965, remember when someone in the neighborhood got a second car, or the neighbor down the street got a new color TV, or someone now had a second TV in their house? Wow, everyone had to have the same! That is how the term 'keeping up with the Joneses' started. Everyone started consuming more than what was really needed to 'live'. And now, well, there are Super HDTV's on the walls in every room, multiple cars in the driveway and garage, and every gadget and electronic available throughout the house. This phenomenon is relatively new, but our whole worldwide economy is now based upon it.

Consumerism then, is the act of spending money on items and services that we use in everyday life. These are usually much more than we actually need to sustain life; they are goods and services that we have been told, especially by advertisers and marketers, that we cannot do without, cannot live without, and we have to keep up with the Joneses. There are some items that we certainly do not want to live without, like toothpaste and deodorant! There are some of the consumption type items that are really everyday necessities, things that we have used, and repurchased, every month or two or three for our entire lives. The difference between one, two, or three months is if you are one of those bulk, warehouse shoppers! If you understand this basic concept, then you will also understand where the Law of Consumerism comes into play.

Since there are numerous goods and services that we will use, run out of, repurchase, over and over again—everything from monthly cell phone subscriptions to everyday hygiene products to gasoline and food—then the only factor to a consumer is the perceived value, in the form of need and convenience, the money being spent, and how well the product or service works and fits into that person's lifestyle. The Law of Consumerism then becomes somewhat "Wal*Mart-ized," meaning the largest retailer of goods and services in the world has built an empire on the words "low cost" or "cheap." In a Wal*Mart-ized world, if you want to compete, you better be able to compete, somewhat, on price. It is not just price alone, but the Law of Consumerism takes price into consideration because of this phenomenon.

At the end of this Industrial Economy, there has been a race to the bottom, all based on price. We are discovering what a huge mistake that is, but it is a fact of life now. You may be able to attract the innovators and maybe even the early adopters without consideration to price or need, but to get to the sweet spot, the early majority, you must take into consideration the Law of Consumerism.

Another major ingredient, especially in the Connection Economy, is trust. Today, many of the top consumer companies in the world have built their business on a value proposition that includes trust in the product or service. The question, though, is whether that trust is real or perceived. Perceived trust occurs when a product or service is popular because that is the way it has always been, because through decades of marketing and advertising, it is what we know, so we trust the product. For example, think Tide Laundry Detergent. Does it mean Tide is the best? Not necessarily. It just meets the Law of Consumerism in price and perceived trust, and, therefore is a product that does over $1 billion a year in sales for Proctor and Gamble. When we discuss some of the differences in various Independent Contractor models later, you will see why so many of the Network Marketing companies with a MLM compensation system are inauthentic because they do not practice the Law of Consumerism, particularly in need, price, and trust. That is a big red flag. The Law of Consumerism affects everything and in this century will become more and more important to understand and practice your business. It is also important to understand that not all businesses are made equally, and not all Business Models deliver the end result that you may be looking for.

A Business Model describes the rationale of how an organization creates, delivers, and captures value (economic, social, or other forms of value). The process of Business Model construction is part of business strategy. In the early history of Business Models it was very typical to define Business Model types such as brick-and-mortar or e-broker. However, these types usually describe only one aspect of the business, most often the revenue model. Therefore, more recent literature on Business Models concentrates on describing Business Models as a whole instead of one most visible aspects.

The following examples provide an overview for various Business Model types that have been in discussion since the invention of the term "Business Model":

- Bricks-and-clicks Business Model

  In the early days of the Internet, (1990's) when the idea of online purchasing was taking hold, innovation added a new stream model to the age old system of transactional business. For thousands of years there was the brick-and-mortar (store front) business, and for a hundred years there was the mail order business. The new stream was online business; now there were three.

Our business lexicon added something that was a new buzz-phrase, bricks-and-clicks or clicks-and-bricks, whichever you like. One of the first official uses was reported to be from a magazine article written in September 1999, reporting an address given by Andy Grove; at that time the chairman of Intel Corporation. He asked the question, "Do you work for a bricks company, a clicks company, or a bricks-and-clicks company?" Basically a bricks-and-clicks business is an enterprise that uses the model by which a company integrates both offline (bricks) and online (clicks) presences. One example of the bricks-and-clicks model is when a chain of stores allows the user to order products online, but lets them pick up their order at a local store.

This model has been evolving over the years with the acceptance by the buying public and with the safety and security of buying online. It is ever-changing, and with Amazon, Inc. recently becoming the second largest retailer in the world, behind Wal*Mart Stores, this model will continue to evolve. We have seen some of those changes very recently with the announcement from Big Box retailers, like Best Buy, Inc., who are not only reducing the size of their 'bricks', to more of a showroom experience, but they are also price matching any other bricks or clicks retailer, the 'Wal*Mart-izing' effect. We have also seen a plethora of action on taxability by local, state, and the federal governments as it relates to online buying. The days of tax free buying online are going...going...gone!

- Collective Business Models

Business organizations or associations typically composed of relatively large numbers of businesses, tradespersons, or professionals in the same or related fields of endeavor, which pools resources, shares information, or provides other benefits for their members. These are sometimes referred to as "cooperatives." The cooperative model is another one which is becoming more relevant in the marketplace today, to be able to compete in the very competitive, global arena in which we live.

- Cutting-out-the middleman Model

  The removal of intermediaries in a supply chain: "cutting out the middleman." Instead of going through traditional distribution channels, which had some type of intermediate (such as a store, distributor, wholesaler, broker, or agent), companies may now deal with every customer directly, for example via the Internet. This model is gaining in popularity and many, many examples exist today of its success, like Netflix. In fact, this model is currently driving the old Industrial Economy crazy. They are so entrenched in their way of business that the efficiencies available today via technological advancements makes this model very attractive.

  This model is sometimes referred to as a "disruptive" Business Model because this model is disrupting the way it has been for hundreds of years during the Industrial Revolution. There are many examples of industries being changed via a disruption of the normal, such as Dell Computers in the personal computer arena, and Netflix in movie rental. Netflix is now taking on legacy TV with their streaming service and allowing the customer to decide how many episodes of a series they want to watch, and when. Phenomenal!

  Another example, as discussed previously, is what Dollar Shave Club has done by cutting out the middlemen. I am confident of many more disruptions to occur in this new Connection Economy.

- Direct sales Model

  Direct selling is marketing and selling products to consumers directly, away from a fixed retail location. Sales are typically made through the party plan, one-to-one demonstrations, and other personal contact arrangements. A text book definition is: "The direct personal presentation, demonstration, and sale of products and services to consumers, usually in their homes or at their jobs." We will discuss this model in more detail in Chapter 11.

- Distribution Business Models, various

  There are so many different distribution type models which have experienced solid growth and threats over the years. And with the advent of globalization and the Internet in the late 20th century, now expanding in this century, these models are under pressure, all the time.

- Fee in, free out Model

  This Business Model works by charging the first client a fee for a service, while offering that service free of charge to subsequent clients.

- Franchise Model

  Franchising is the practice of using another firm's successful Business Model. For the franchisor, the franchise is an alternative to building chain stores to distribute goods and avoid investment and liability over a chain. The franchisor's success is the success of the franchisees. The franchisee is said to have a greater incentive than a direct employee because he or she has a direct stake in the business. We will discuss this one in detail in Chapter 10.

- MLM Business Model

  The term "Multi-Level Marketing" is one of the most misunderstood of all the different types of Business Models. It is not a Business Model at all, but a way of compensation for a Network Marketing company. Companies that have a MLM compensation system have levels of distribution based upon how large a business is, or the position within the business, or when someone started. It comes in all shapes and sizes and must be scrutinized closely to see if they really do fit the Law of Consumerism. We will discuss this compensation system in more detail in Chapter 11.

- Network Marketing Business Model

  We will also discuss this model in much more detail in the coming chapters. The Network Marketing model is one in which, usually as an Independent Contractor for a company's goods or services, you are able to build a distribution system, a book of business, by adding customers and training and mentoring a sales force to do the same. What makes all Network Marketing companies different is tied directly to the way the Independent Contractors compensation works.

- Freemium Business Model

  This Business Model works by offering basic Web services, or a basic downloadable digital product, for free, while charging a premium for advanced or special features.

Other examples of Business Models are:

- Auction Business Model
- Loyalty Business Models
- Online auction Business Model
- Online content Business Model
- Pyramid scheme Business Model
- Subscription Business Model

And there are even more. The above are just the most identifiable.

In your quest to find Perfect Business Inc., it is important that you do not *buy yourself a job.*

As I have mentioned before, there can be a fine line between self-employed and unemployed. Just as well, there can be little distinction between working for a boss and being your own boss. One of the big advantages of working for a boss is that when the shift is over, you can go home. When you are self-employed in the wrong model, it can be a nightmare of endless days and nights strung end to end leaving you wishing you had kept your 'real' job.

Perhaps one of the best examples of the fine line that exists is America's favorite fast food. The McDonald's Corporation is one of the first icons people see when they begin to look at a method or pathway to be independent. The temptation is simple: a big company with almost guaranteed success wrapped in a tried and proven system. Today over 33,500 restaurants dot the world.

It is no longer inexpensive to get into however; you must pay as much as a million dollars or more to get your franchise. In the beginning, it was a simple process, reasonably-priced, and easy to learn. As the years passed, it has become ever more difficult, with stringent qualifications, enormous franchise fees, and endless contracts and agreements with guidelines that carry strict consequences if not followed properly.

Even after you become a franchisee with McDonald's, you have only purchased a system; the McDonald's Corporation owns the real estate. Many people do not realize that you pay for the equipment and materials, but the M company owns the dirt. McDonald's boasts of being one of the largest holders of prime real estate in the world.

Yet still, by the thousands, people bid and struggle to get an opportunity for this perceived pathway to independence. Many people wait for years just to get on the list to be considered as a franchisee. Today, 80 percent of the 33,500 restaurants are owned by franchisees, totaling about 2,200 people. If you calculated the average, it would be about 13 restaurants per franchise holder. People simply cannot make it on only one franchise in today's environment. People think that one franchise will make it, but it does not.

We saw the same thing happen with franchising at Circle K. It was an extremely expensive endeavor to get a Circle K franchise location open and operating: the gasoline tanks and system alone could put you back one million dollars. For those who were able to open a store, they essentially bought themselves a job with an enormous amount of work and headaches. And at the end of the day, if that franchisee earned $40,000 to $50,000 in income for the year, they did well. The average income in the U.S. in 2012 by the U.S. Census Bureau was $49,445, so as a single store operator, you have essentially bought yourself a job to maintain the average of the middle class salary level, with no leverage or freedom.

The point is that people are not investing into their freedom; they are simply buying themselves a job. While it is possible to obtain time freedom through careful structuring, training, trusting, and monitoring of your businesses, it is rarely done. Most franchise owners I have known or dealt with were burning the candle not only on the ends and the middle but had essentially simply thrown the candle into the fireplace.

Anyone can obtain money; time freedom requires leverage. For the past 18 years, I have gone to the same drycleaner, the one I spoke of in the previous chapter. The week they closed to take a vacation, I pondered how little of a difference there is between working for some company and owning your own small business, since neither offer you time and freedom leverage.

Like the surgeon, no matter how well paid you are, if you do not cut, you do not earn. You may make a living, and in many cases a good living, being in your own professional field or owning your own franchise but if you do not have time freedom to go along with the money, you are just an employee in a higher income tax bracket.

At the time of this writing, I am preparing over the next few months to take three different trips, with one being to Hawaii, all because of creating leverage.

A properly leveraged business allows you to enjoy time freedom along with the money. To understand this, let me explain a law that you must apply to your business plan. If this law fails to find ground with you, you may wish to consider a different avenue. It is often called a law or principle of the harvest.

The law of the harvest comes from farming, but it applies exactly to your Perfect Model Inc. business. It is an exciting concept, and it can be accelerated, but never circumvented.

The farmer in the wintertime is always busy. Keeping snow off the roof, maintaining the farm equipment, feeding the livestock, storing up seed for spring, and plowing fertilizer into the fields for the future. The farmer is not making money, in fact there is a good chance they are living on borrowed, or saved-up money or stores. This can be likened to you working now in a regular nine to five job, but yearning and working to become independent.

Come springtime, the workload gets even tougher. The farmer is plowing, planting, fertilizing, and working sometimes from before dawn to late into the night. This is a critical time when the farmer rarely goes bowling or takes time off for anything. Also, the farmer is not paid much, if anything. This time can be compared to you expending some time and money to invest into your new business venture, when the capital of money and time are flowing away from you as you acquire your venture.

Summer seems to drag on forever. Endless work to keep the crops growing, the weeds in check, and the equipment tuned up for the most important months ahead, Fall! Still the farmer is not making much money, if any at all. This summertime can be equated to you working through the start-up months, plowing through the leads, and enduring the turn-downs that are part of the learning curve and the growing first cycles of your business.

When the day of harvest finally arrives, everyone celebrates. The crops are brought in and a feast is prepared. Later there is so much harvest that much is taken to the market and sold. Often there is so much that even a surplus is stored away for winter, and some might even be given away! These are the months of abundance from the long months of hard work. In late fall, with a fat bank account and a full barn, the farmer begins to prepare for winter where the cycle will begin again. That is where the similarity ends between your business and the farmers, if you select the correct Business Model, one with a true residual income potential that we will discuss throughout this book.

Once you are here, and it may take a year or a few years, it is at this point, if you are in a truly leveraged business, your business will grow while you are on vacation. It is out of your hands now, and success is no longer a matter of what you do. Your efforts simply determine the speed in which you are increasing.

With a basic maintenance program you will remain in the fall state of abundance. It is said that in your system of business, the work you do in the beginning is ludicrous when compared to the money you make. Over time, however, the little work you will do for the abundant money you will make will seem equally as ludicrous. Here is an illustration of what I mean:

W	W	W	W	W
O	O	O	O	$
R	R	R	$	$
K	K	$	$	$

I once heard someone say that many times in building a residual income business we do the work, at the beginning especially, that people just are not willing to do, to enjoy a life later on that most people will never enjoy. In other words, sometimes you work hard today, without being immediately compensated for that work, in order to live a life later that others will not because of the residual income you now enjoy. Rarely can you quit working, as we discussed earlier, passive income is not what is readily available, but over time you can control your schedule, your time, and your life, with a well-built residual income stream.

If you have ever read the book *Outliers: The Story of Success* by Malcolm Gladwell, he states that to become proficient at something, it takes around 10,000 hours. Now, if you had, say, 20 hours a week to begin putting into a "Plan B," a Network Marketing business, and it takes 10,000 hours to become proficient, then it will take you many years to become an expert at your business. After I read this book, I went back, analyzed my business, and it was right at the seven year mark of my current business that I became extremely confident, proficient and began earning almost double yearly what I had the first six years. This is why I am always amazed when someone decides to begin a Network Marketing business and then quits after a very short amount of time because they were not earning the thousands of dollars they thought.

That logic usually comes from the hype of inauthentic Network Marketing businesses and their front men. It is just that, hype. So, many times, when dump-trucks worth of money do not just miraculously show up at the front door after a few months, these posers and amateurs quit their Network Marketing business and start telling others how "those things do not work." Well, I have seen many work, and work successfully for the professional, the ones who do not buy into the hype, who actually analyze whether the business itself is authentic, or inauthentic (does it meet the law of consumerism?), then treat it like a business, understanding that to become proficient, new skills will need to be learned, and new practices garnered, about 10,000 hours in all to become successful, just like the law of the harvest.

Today many companies, especially Network Marketing companies, have jump start/quick start programs that can help you to begin earning income immediately. But the big money and the time freedom, the residual income you will get will be from performance over time, if you have selected the correct vehicle.

All of us who have made significant residual income can relate to this principle, and we empathize with the new person starting out. All we can say or do is encourage you to remember that it is a marathon, not a sprint. If you are emotionally all in, then you are providing a service to others that enhances lives. Set your goals to reflect the outcome of your efforts and the enjoyment and fulfillment you will have as your business grows. And never, ever quit!

So to recap this important principle of the harvest: choose wisely the company you will build, and make sure it has the indicators that secure leverage; make certain that you are not simply buying yourself a job; and, most importantly, do not quit! Work hard through the startup phase of your business with an eye on the harvest. Cultivate the new organization as it grows. Cultivate, do not just throw fertilizer on it!

Chapter 9

It Must Be Truly

"A problem is something that can be solved.
A fact of life is something that must be accepted."

– John Maxwell

The Business you start, join, invent, and so on, is one which must be on the "B" side of the cash flow quadrant. If residual income is our dream, our lottery, our sweepstakes, then you cannot be an "E" or an "S" and expect to be obtaining residual income. We all wish for it, hope for it, dream about it, and buy our lotto tickets each week to try to obtain it. Residual income or what some call "mailbox money," is simply income arriving that we are not trading our precious lifetime for. It is a check in the mail.

We hear every day that it is available to us if we are willing to roll up our sleeves and work for it, but we know by sad experience that most people will never have it in their lifetime, except for the little retirement check when we have passed our prime years of health and energy.

Actors and recording artists inadvertently employed all of the principles that I am now going to share with you; they did not even realize that they were following a necessary protocol to get their check in the mail. Let me explain: I call it the "truly principle".

Truly Unique

First, in order to create a residual income stream or royalty that is mailed to you, you must have a unique product. The recording artist is unique; their music is unique to the performer or a genre that is currently popular, or at least popular with a large segment of the buying population. Likewise, you must have a good quality product that is not readily available on the shelf of the corner convenience store.

Today's consumer goods marketplace is dominated by big-box superstores with enormous buying power or the online e-tailers with razor thin margins. There is no way you can have a long term success and, thus, a successful income with products that people can find somewhere else a lot cheaper—especially if they are me-too commodity type products that compete only on price. In this environment, there simply is no room for the would-be start up entrepreneur to compete unless you have a product or service that is truly unique and available only from you.

Do not be hoodwinked by fancy ads and marketing that you can make it long term and in a solid business venture on a trend or fad business pitch. Avoid the temptation! Use this book as a guide to accurately vet the sales presentation that catches your eye.

Truly Essential and Consumable

Think about the consumer goods that are essential in your life. Take a look around your home, for instance. If you cut out everything you did not need to survive, you would be left with the bare essentials. Your home would look very different, perhaps like a vintage 1960 atomic bomb shelter. These remaining goods that you would be seeing are the kinds of product that are *truly* recession proof. Companies that manufacture these kinds of products are usually very large, rock solid, blue-chip companies. You, too, want this kind of product, plus the last point: unique.

Although the market has been dominated for generations by a few multi-billion dollar companies, there are other large businesses out there looking for you to represent their unique, quality products and services. They do not require large investments and in many cases no big inventory requirement.

Truly Reasonably Priced

There are many companies touting some kind of miracle product that can help someone grow back a limb that they lost back in the Viet Nam War era; some juice, anti-aging elixir or miracle breakthrough cream, potion or lotion that comes from a root growing in the darkest cave of a remote island. Beware! These are flags that simply should remind you that breakthrough science is easily vetted, and the more exclusive the idea is the more the reality check should be engaged.

One flag is price. It is a big flag and should be given serious consideration. It tracks very closely with the Law of Consumerism. When you are confronted with this kind of product, take a closer look to see if it is really the hope of the opportunity that is driving the enterprise as opposed to the true efficacy of the product. Will people purchase it because they really trust it, need it, use it, and find value—especially for what they have to pay—when it is compared to products in the general marketplace?

There is an old saying that goes "If you want to dine with the classes, you have got to deal with the masses." Face it—the masses will not shell out long for overpriced products, especially non-essential ones. The landscape is littered with companies who lost the perspective of what consumerism is all about. It is about value, trust, and perception and, in the mind of the consumer, many times value and perception are all about price. Yes, it is not always fair, but it is the Wal*Mart-izing of the world! In today's economy, the masses are looking for the best bang for their consumer dollar. They only have so much money in their budget and if your product(s) can offer better value than what they are already buying, you will create a real formula for long term customers. This loyalty helps to guarantee your true, residual income.

Truly Convenient

When Netflix started sending movies right to your home in the mail, they became a very disruptive Business Model. What was the net result? Most small mom-and-pop video rental stores are now out of business. Even the giant market leaders like Blockbuster in the United States or Rogers in Canada have had to drastically change their Business Models to compete. Blockbuster has now announced that they will completely cease operations. Some are out of business because they either did not see Netflix coming or they failed to stay competitive with the convenience trend.

For better or for worse, our society is a convenience-trend society. Everyone wants to be served: "easier," "more convenient," "simpler," "transparent," and "painless" are the buzzwords of today's busy, modern lifestyle. If your products are part of the truly effective and convenient trend, you are at an advantage.

If you have products that can be easily ordered and delivered direct to the customer, right where they use them, you can participate in a disruptive Business Model for the traditional shopping headache, and have the formula for repeat business and again, creating that true residual income.

This is a really important point in our Connection Economy. Technology is changing everything; do you see it?

In continuing our quest to find permanent residual income, we can take our quest for *Truly* aspects of residual income into identifying the frauds and fads.

Truly Sustainable—Not Just a Fad

Remember the Hula Hoop? You should; they have been around since 5th century Greece. In the 1950s though, they became a fad, and a big one. Remember the Pet Rock, Chia-Pet, and the Cabbage Patch kids? Who still has a box of Pogs in the back of a closet shelf?

Each one of these probably provoke a fond memory and causes you a little smile; I know they do me. Remember waiting a little too long to purchase that He-Man doll at Christmastime and your willingness to pay a premium if you could find one from a street vendor?

All of these products were incredible success stories—but only for a season. They were all flash trends that came and went. You can still find shadows of these products, but the frenzy of their emergence into the market and their quick demise are lessons to help us find our true residual income. They were true fads that came, and went!

We have seen the same trends with home-based businesses as well. Whether it was water filters, alarm systems, personal websites, travel clubs, or the expensive fruit juice of the week, each provided only those that joined at the very beginning the ability to enjoy any type of wealth creation. In these fleeting businesses, the emphasis is on getting in on the ground floor…rather than creating a truly-real business that can stand the test of time. They simply could not provide a sustainable Business Model in a sustainable industry. Unless you are fortunate enough to perfectly pick the next fad, or get in on the ground or, even better, basement, floor and ride the wave until it disappears, there is no way to ever create true long term, stable, residual income with these fad businesses.

There are, of course, technology products as well. Over the past decade where once we kept a cell phone for two or three years, today it is not unusual to upgrade each quarter. If you are old enough to remember the Commodore 64 personal computer or the Atari video game system, you have most likely been mesmerized multiple times or even overwhelmed over the past several decades by technology advancements. From Pong to Pac-Man to virtual 3D technologies, one thing is for sure: technology never rests. Manufactures all agree that by the time a new item is released to the public it is probably already going, or is, obsolete. Tying your financial future to technology that will soon be replaced or enhanced, most likely by competitive companies, will not provide long term residual income.

Truly In-Budget- Not luxury or impulse

Your product or service must blend into the lives of your customers without disrupting their budgets. How often does the average consumer buy a diamond ring or expensive watch? Can you even imagine a motorcycle or flat screen television being shipped to people on a monthly basis? It is absurd. When considering a business that can create true on-going residual income, you must find a product that can tap into the day to day essential needs of your customers. Every consideration must be given to blending your items into your customer's daily budget through replacement money: exchanging dollars they already spend with your products which will ideally reduce their expense and improve their lives in the process.

Also important is having products that create loyalty. If you have to constantly resell your product or service over and over, or worse yet, get a new customer for each sale because your product is not consumable, then you will never have true on-going residual income. Even some of the most lucrative professions that offer a good six figure income potential such as real estate, usually do not create residual income. Realtors find out quickly that once they sell a house, they are unemployed until the next sale, which at most times is too far apart. Don't confuse great income with residual income. Even a brain surgeon needs to continue working to keep generating their revenue.

Truly In Control

There are no margins in selling someone else's product! A friend of mine decided to open a storefront where he was selling the landline phone, Internet, cell phone and satellite services of the local technology companies. I asked him at the time what his proforma looked like since I knew how difficult it would be to sell others products with already wire thin margins. He said he would make it work and that he has. No additional income for any employees, he must try to do everything himself, working umpteen hours a day, never seeing his family. There are no margins when you sell someone else's product or service!

Your business should be in complete control over the pipeline from conception of the idea to consumption by the end customer. A company that is some kind of middle-man is dangerous to longevity. Such companies are particularly vulnerable to competitors stealing away ideas and resources.

Having complete control of manufacturing and distribution, from raw materials to the equipment, the supply, and even to the land and the buildings, ensures that you have total quality and value control. This eliminates the potential of weak links or disrupted supply of ingredients and finished products delivered to your customer-consumers. It also ensures that you can remain price competitive in the marketplace, with some margins to work with. This also builds enormous confidence in your presentation when talking to potential clients. If you goal is long term residual income, look only for businesses that control 90 percent, and preferably *all* of the process from idea to end customers consumption.

If the product is digital, then it really should be something that you came up with. Selling other products via affiliate programs will bring in a little income, but certainly will not provide a long lasting, true residual-style income.

Truly Leveraged

We are told by our financial advisors to make our money work for us. This is a great concept if you have money to invest. But, what we are doing here is finding a way to get that money to invest. We want and need the residual income to do that. This is a common dilemma for our time—we only have so many hours in each day to put into our jobs, businesses, or careers. Once we have maxed those hours we have also maxed our earning potential.

We will review a few more examples to clarify what unlimited leverage potential is and what it is not. If you own a small café with three tables, you can easily measure the number of chairs you have for customers by the maximum amount they are likely to spend from your menu items and then multiply that times the hours and days you are open for business. That maximum income potential cannot be exceeded except to expand the entire model.

For another example, say that you own rental properties and you take care of marketing them, renting them and cleaning them. You do not have residual income as you have just created a full time job that requires a great deal of effort on your part. There is a fine line between self employment and unemployment; do you own your business, or does it own you?

If for some reason you were unable to work due to accident or illness, then your revenue could be severely affected. You could hire employees and pay others to do this work and, as long as you did not have any weak links in the chain, this could create an on-going residual income, albeit very fragile. You will, however, have to have the money to invest in the first place as I mentioned earlier. You will have to pay the management company a healthy percentage and hope the housing market does not suffer some type of economic downturn or complete crash, which happens on a fairly cyclical basis. Even professionals such as doctors, attorneys, architects, and engineers are at the mercy of trading their expertise for income. If for any reason that is disrupted, so is their income. If the surgeon does not cut, he is not paid.

We will go one step further: most small business owners find themselves struggling to find anyone that cares as much about their business as they do. It is their baby, their enterprise. The net result is long hours, little if any time off, and the stresses of making every decision every day to ensure long term viability.

It is imperative at the outset of your search for the perfect Business Model, to see that there is a program of complete leveraging of all of the above mentioned obstacles to your success. The key words you can use to sum up this application of leverage is duplication.

Truly Duplicatable

You have heard it said that "if it was that easy then everyone would be doing it." The author of this line had probably just finished their Master's Degree at Harvard or created an operating system used by every PC on the planet.

Over the past 20 years, would you have rather been the owner of Microsoft or Apple? When looked at each, many would say that Apple is the bigger success story here. I would disagree. You see, Apple makes stuff, Microsoft licenses stuff. There is a big difference here. Microsoft actually has had the most leverage as a company due to its platform being offered on just about every PC made. Microsoft has devised a duplicatable system that pays them an enormous residual-style revenue stream. Apple, on the other hand, must come up with the latest, greatest, newest technology, over and over again, and sell it to the public. Microsoft has been like a machine and Apple, even though very successful, has had to work a whole lot harder. The challenge for Microsoft is how to stay relative, over time, with the advancement of technology and especially, open source software like Ubuntu and Linux.

The reality is that for most businesses or individuals that have created residual wealth, it was difficult and very few have ever been blessed with the abilities, intelligence, or circumstances to make it happen. The goal then is for anyone striving to create true on-going long term income to create a system of success that can allow the average person to succeed at whatever level they aspire too, based solely on a strong desire and the ability to follow a proven duplicatable process. This process must be universally available and easy to teach and replicate. You must spend the time to evaluate the system you want to use to create success for average folks and the ease of which it can be duplicated.

As mentioned earlier, there are companies that can and actually prefer to do all of the things the average soul cannot do. That is the secret, the arcane or esoteric information that is right in front of everyone, yet they miss it. With a good and correctly developed system, the ordinary person can achieve extraordinary heights of success.

Franchisors have created duplicatable systems, which is why the franchise Business Model exists today. We will take this up more in chapter 10.

Truly Universal—No territories, no boundaries

We will conduct a short poll to see if you currently have residual income.

Are you tied to an office? Can you take off when you wish? Can you leave for extended periods? Can you take your family when you travel? Do you have to wake up at a certain time each day? Do you always know what day it is? Do you have a 'vacation' time you must adhere to? Do you have a uniform or clothing protocol? Can you be fired, reported, or reviewed? Can you be promoted or demoted? Is your boss in your mirror?

For most people, the hope of earning a strong, on-going income while enjoying a sunset swim in the Caribbean or taking a stroll along a Tuscan village lane is but a dream. Your new business needs to remove two sets of boundaries that are very important to your achievement of strolling a shady lane in the Italian countryside. One, you must not have a boundary where you conduct your business, within reason. Two, you must be able to conduct your business from your home, or on Sunset Beach, Hawaii. This is why being in Quadrant 'E' or 'S' will not deliver to you a wonderful life filled with your passion and purpose on this earth.

Today, more than ever before, it is possible to have a more global business. With international trade a global reality and with the Internet to develop and conduct business in real time from anywhere in the world, there has never in the history of man, been a better time for you to find Perfect Business, Inc and build it to create that elusive dream and turn it into a reality.

Your business must afford you these two important windows of effort: sell anywhere, work from anywhere.

Lifestyle, peace of mind, security, and legacy are all by-products of true residual income. We all want this; we would all enjoy this; so why are these elements so elusive? Is it because we are not talented? Do we lack the ability to act, sing, sell, or invent things? We can use these as excuses as they are probably very good answers for us, but the biggest obstacle is simply lack of an honest opportunity that we *can* do; opportunity that is not dependent on when you get in, gimmicks in the marketplace, or fads that come and go. You want a shot that is not selling potions and lotions of questionable efficacy or technologies that fleeting tempt you as the next big thing.

No, residual wealth is possible when you find the true opportunity that falls within the key factors of this book and particularly this chapter you are reading. There is another key element in your success, and that will be discussed in detail later, but for now I will just say this. You must have a company managed by quality, upstanding, and honest people who clearly know and present that you are the deciding factor for their success. If you do not succeed, they know that they cannot succeed.

Chapter 10

Deeper Dive Into A Few Types of Businesses

"Though no one can go back and make a brand new start, anyone can start from now and make a brand new ending."

– Carl Bard

For the sake of keeping this book manageable, we are not going to delve into all the different types of Business Models discussed in Chapter 8. We are, however, going to discuss the ones which someone picking up this book would be interested in. This is really for those souls who say, "Okay, So What Now?" Maybe you are from what was a two-income household which just became a one-income household due to a job loss; maybe you are a Mom wanting to contribute to the family's earning potential, maybe you are a Gen-Y college grad finding dead end job opportunities after college (or the disdain in actually working a 9 to 5-er!); or maybe you are one of those so called "Beached White Males," a term used by the media over the past few years to identify those ex-Corporate Executive Types, mostly Baby Boomers, who use to drive the BMW's and are now BWM's in real life! Whatever is it for you, my goal is to give you enough ammunition here, enough logic, to be able to make an informed decision on the potential livelihood for the rest of your life. I am so fortunate to have gone through some early adoption of many of the principles here, I had my share of failure, and would love nothing more than to give you some shortcuts in finding your "what now."

I am assuming that if you are reading this, you have decided that being an employee of someone else's is most likely a dead end, either because there does not seem to be anything out there for you, or you are overqualified, or any other of the various potential scenarios. If, however, you do decide that being employed by someone is for you, then be the best you can be, be a difference-maker. I would highly suggest picking up a copy of Seth Godin's, *Linchpin: Are You Indispensable?* and *The Icarus Deception.* Both of these books discuss how to become indispensable, how to be the best you can be, how to be an artist in your field. Even as an entrepreneur, both of these books are excellent reads to really get a good grasp on the new economy, this Connection Economy.

You may also currently be an employee or a small business owner looking for an exit strategy. There are many others doing the exact same thing these days: looking at an exit strategy while still working where they are right now. Starting something part-time in order to have some options down the road is a noble thing to do these days. However, it takes some real discipline to manage a work schedule, family obligations, and a new part time enterprise, so understand what it takes. If you have a family, make sure they understand and everyone buys in. Understand also that you may have to give up something in order to reach your goals.

You are most likely looking at maybe starting your own business as a small business owner, whether it be a traditional small business, franchising, working from home, or network marketing, so we will discuss them!

Self-Employment

Starting a business is not for everyone. Being self-employed is very different than being an employee. And remember, according to our Cash Flow Quadrant we discussed earlier, self-employment, with everything that goes along with it, may still put you on the wrong side of the ledger, the S Quadrant. Now, I am not saying that you cannot get wealthy and have some time freedom starting up a traditional-style business and being self-employed, but I am saying that for 90 percent of the people that do, they have effectively bought themselves a job with no freedom whatsoever. And some people find it impossible to adjust to the differences between being an employee of someone else and now being self-employed. So let us see if you have the necessary entrepreneurial mindset to become self-employed. These are the six traits that I think encapsulate the ways you have to think and behave if you want to make a successful transition from being employed in someone else's business to starting a business of your own.

You have to be flexible

If you start a business, you no longer have "one" job with clearly defined duties and responsibilities. You will suddenly have multiple jobs, which will be often interrupted by unforeseen crises. Many employees are used to having days filled with predictable activities; many self-employed people do not.

And once you start a business, there is nowhere to pass the buck. As an employee, you may be used to passing problems up along the food chain or not be very involved in decision making. As a self-employed business owner, you are the one who will have to deal with whatever the crisis is and solve the problem. You are the one who will have to make the decisions.

You have to be a self-motivated initiator

When you are an employee, Quadrant E, other people tell you what to do, either directly or indirectly. You get used to having your actions directed by others. But you have to direct your own actions as a small business owner. You cannot just sit there and hope that maybe some clients stroll in or that someone will drop by out of the blue with inventory for your retail store. No one is going to drop work on your desk or point out what needs to be done. For many people who try to become self-employed and start businesses after having a long-term full-time job, this is the hardest adjustment to make.

You have to be able to recognize opportunities and go after them

Most employees do what they are assigned to do. There is someone else who is assigned to look out for opportunities, either a boss in a small business, or perhaps a sales department or a managerial team in a large corporation. If you start a business, you need to be the one constantly watching for opportunities—and be able to recognize them when you see them. It might be a small opportunity, such as the chance to pick up a new client, or a large one, such as getting your product on the shelves in a large retail chain, but as a small business owner, you have to keep scanning the horizon yourself and positioning yourself to benefit from the opportunities that you find. As an employee, you may be used to operating in a head-down position; if you are going to start a business and become successfully self-employed, you need to start operating in the head-up position.

When you are self-employed, you have to be able to plan ahead

Your last job may have involved no planning at all, as that was someone else's job. Or perhaps your job involved planning on a localized level, such as planning a particular project. If you want to start a business, you need to develop expertise in both short-term and long-range planning; it is about to become a big part of your life.

When you start a business, one of your first tasks will be to work through a business plan. As your business becomes operational, you will find that this plan, however detailed, needs to be revised and that other plans need to be created, as you work towards the long-range goals that you have set for your business. From following someone else's plan as an employee, you have to learn how to create the plans yourself and adapt the plans to changing circumstances.

You need to be prepared to put in a constant and consistent effort

We have all seen employees who are just going through the motions, or who were just putting in the time until retirement. You do not need to be a co-worker to know who these people are. As a customer or client you can tell, too. Bluntly, starting a business takes energy, and you need to be able to give it 100 percent. You cannot afford to just coast along, or go through the motions, if you are running a business. Your customer or clients need to know that you are devoting 100 percent of your talent or skill or attention to them, and they will go elsewhere if they do not feel this is the case.

Worse, you need to deliver this constant and consistent effort without the employee safety net. Many employees are used to being able to call in sick and have someone else cover their job, for instance. As a self-employed business owner, you will have to go in and give it your best effort no matter how you feel or close up shop if you do not have employees who can fill in. You can also say goodbye to the holidays that many employees enjoy, both the annual certain number of weeks and the statutory holidays, at least until your business is established to the point that you can manage your own time.

You have to be able to deal with uncertainty

As a self-employed entrepreneur, there is no guarantee that the products or services you offer will be in demand six months from now.

There is no guarantee that your customers will pay their bills on time or even pay them at all. There is no guarantee that your current big client, who seems to be perfectly happy with your work, will not just drop you next week. There is actually no guarantee that you will make any income this month or the month after. For many ex-employees who are used to having a pay check arrive regularly every two weeks, the uncertainty of being self-employed is very difficult to deal with.

When I started a consulting business, the first six to eight months were like a sledge hammer had hit my head. I had such a hard time readjusting to my new lifestyle. I mean, I had a tight schedule for over 20 years; I knew where I was to be, had a calendar, employees, others I was responsible to and for. It literally took me months to change my mindset from employee to self-employed.

Are you still asking, "How do I start a business?" Good! Because the point of this is not to scare you off, but to make you aware of how you have to readjust your thinking to make the transition from employee to self-employed business owner. Hopefully as you read through this list of traits you need in order to become successfully self-employed, you were saying to yourself, "I can do this." Because every one of the traits I have listed here is an attitude or behavior that can be learned, and when it comes to being self-employed, awareness is more than half the battle.

Desire, resolve, commitment, passion, purpose, and an understanding that failure is not an option!

Being an Independent Contractor

An Independent Contractor is an individual or business that provides services to another individual or business; it is, in fact, being self-employed. The Independent Contractor is a separate business entity and is not considered an employee. Interestingly enough, the Independent Contractor, depending upon the alignment with a company, can be in the 'S' Quadrant, or the 'B' Quadrant; remember, it is the 'B' Quadrant that can produce true leverage.

Sometimes, it is not a straightforward matter to determine who is an Independent Contractor and who should be classified as an employee. To make that determination, the IRS in the U.S.A. advises taxpayers to look at three aspects of the employment arrangement: financial control, behavioral control, and relationship between the parties. While some

Independent Contractors may work for a number of different organizations throughout the year, there are also many who retain Independent Contractor status even though they work for the same organization for the entire year.

Generally speaking, Independent Contractors retain control over their schedule and number of hours worked, jobs accepted, and performance of their job. In addition, they may have a major investment in equipment, furnish all their own supplies, provide their own insurance, repairs, and all other expenses related to their business. They may also perform a special service that is not in the normal course of business of the employer. This contrasts with the situation for regular employees, who usually work at the schedule required by the employer and whose performance is directly supervised by the employer. However, many companies—particularly in the freight transport industry—specify the contractor's schedule, require purchase of vehicles from the company, and prohibit work for other companies.

Examples of Independent Contractors would include professional athletes, real estate agents, accountants, hair stylist, truck drivers, and anyone representing a Network Marketing company.

At the end of the year Independent Contractors are supplied with a Form 1099 by the company they provide a service for and are required to pay income taxes, Social Security, and Medicare taxes. We will cover more on taxes in Chapter 13.

Independent Contractors can either be in the transactional income system or the residual income system. Realtors, for example, are in transactional income: they are unemployed every time they sell a house. In other words, selling a house and earning three percent on the sale is just that, a one-time sale; I have not seen too many people buy another house the next month! It takes a great client list with ongoing sales to be successful.

Being self-employed, or being an Independent Contractor takes additional motivation, organization, and discipline. If that is not you, you will probably be better as a Quadrant E person, at hourly or salary employment.

Now that you know that you are the kind of person who can start a business and run it successfully, where do you go from here?

Traditional Start-up Bricks-and-Mortar

Starting up a new traditional bricks-and-mortar business surely is not for the timid. It takes capital (usually about three to five years of working capital), knowledge of the industry, rock solid projections, and proformas and a business plan. As we discussed in Chapter 5, this type of business puts you in the 'S' Quadrant, and so it is purely transactional. Be willing to put your heart and soul into it, and make sure you have the passion, are emotionally all in, for whatever it is you want to do.

I have seen on many occasions a person want to start a traditional style business not because of really being passionate, but with the sole purpose of hoping it will work so as to be able to franchise the idea down the road. Not a bad idea, as long as you have the wherewithal to stick with it until it can possibly duplicate.

I know of a gentlemen who did exactly this: he opened one of these new self-serve yogurt shops with the intent to begin franchising his shops all over town. He spent three years perfecting the Business Model, working obscene hours, dealing with all the things business owners deal with, from liability insurances to taxes to benefits and payroll. He finally felt he was ready and began to advertise the franchising of his brand and system. Now, he was about to go from transactional income to residual income based on royalties paid to him monthly by others.

What he did not anticipate was the amount of work involved in being a store owner and now, franchisor too, with all the headaches that come with people who have bought into your idea not making it and complaining all the time. You see, what really happened is that this fad, self-serve yogurt shops, started popping up everywhere; it seemed like there was one on every block, and it began to erode the performance of each shop.

It makes me think about the question I would get at Circle K quite often: "Why are there two stores, each Circle K's, right across the street from each other?" And the response: "Well, better to be one of our stores than a 7-11!" Yes, we would buy properties that we were worried might be purchased by the competition and sometimes build stores on them, sometimes just own the property, and sometimes deed-restrict them, as a way to manage the competition! It is a tough, competitive world out there these days!

New Connection Economy Information

You will find all kinds of formulas on the Internet today to being a digital guru, publishing and selling online in our new digital, informational society. There are so many different ways to capitalize on the Connection Economy that we could do just a book on these new opportunities. What is so important is to find ways to monetize your ideas. Many people today think that, because of the Internet, they just have to throw something out there and watch it work. Unfortunately, it just does not work that way. There are companies who still advertise workshops about how to set up your own Internet store, and bundles of money will come your way. For a fee, they will help you with the website, the merchant account, and the education in having customer show up at your site, and off you go.

But, once again, as has been mentioned throughout, unless you have some control over the product or service, unless it fits the law of consumerism, unless you have something of value that cannot be found at the local store, unless you have a massive list to market to, the chances of online success are slim to none. Many had become Amazon resellers, or affiliates, until recently, when the online tax changes have caused Amazon, as well as other large online retailers, to reevaluate some of their affiliate programs.

And affiliate programs abound in the marketplace. Come up with something of value that the masses want and need, put it out there for others to sell online for you, allow them to market to their list and pay the affiliate a commission for directing the traffic and sales to your product or service. Usually, however, these affiliate program, such as what Amazon has, pay you one time for the delivery of a customer, after that, the customer is "owned" by Amazon, for example. No true residual income there. There are many programs, though, that teach the how-to, where to go to find programs, and how to build massive lists, without spam, to market to.

Over the years, and basically because of email spam, we are all seeing a reduction of email open rates, which hurts anyone and everyone attempting to market online. For example, and as has happened to me various times, when some author with an affiliate program through their publisher writes a new book, five to ten emails are sent to the email lists promoting that new product. I sometimes feel bad for the ones I did not open but it was the exact same email sent out over and over again.

Franchising

Franchising is a Business Model in which many different owners share a single brand name. A parent company allows entrepreneurs to use the company's strategies and trademarks; in exchange, the franchisee pays an initial fee and royalties based on revenues. The parent company also provides the franchisee with support, including advertising and training, as part of the franchising agreement.

Franchising is a faster, cheaper form of expansion than adding company-owned stores because it costs the parent company much less when new stores are owned and operated by a third party. On the flip side, potential for revenue growth is more limited because the parent company will only earn a percentage of the earnings from each new store. Seventy different industries use the franchising Business Model, and according to the International Franchising Association, the sector earns more than $1.5 trillion in revenues each year.

Believe it or not, back in the late 1950s and early 1960s, franchising as a Business Model was almost deemed an illegal way of business by the Congress of the U.S.A. Franchising came within just a few votes of being outlawed, and look at it today! Where would we be without the franchising Business Model? Thousands of entrepreneurs made it big in franchising, and still do today.

The only negative now is the cost involved in opening a franchise and, depending upon the industry, the cluttering of the marketplace. There is quite a saturation that has happened over time within many industries, like fast food. Oh, so you want to obtain a McDonald's franchise? In order to qualify for a conventional franchise, you have to have $250,000 not borrowed. Your total costs to open the restaurant, though, will be anywhere from $600,000 to $1,500,000, which goes to paying for the building, equipment, etc. Forty percent of this cost has to be from your own non-borrowed funds.

You will pay an initial franchise fee of $45,000 directly to McDonald's. The other costs go to suppliers, so this is the only upfront fee you pay to McDonald's. Then, you will go through a rigorous nine-month training period where you will learn about the McDonald's way of doing things—such as their standards for quality, service, value, formulas, and specifications for menu items, their method of operation, and inventory control-techniques. You will have to agree to operate the restaurant from a single location, usually for 20 years, following their guidelines for decor, signage, layout, and everything else that makes McDonald's what the public knows and loves.

Once you have completed training and are ready to go, McDonald's will offer you a location they have already developed. McDonald's is actually one of the largest owners of quality real estate in the world. When asked once about what business they were in, one of the executives said "Why, we are in the real estate business." What a truism!

Once you are operating your store, you will pay McDonald's a monthly fee of four percent of your sales *and* either a flat base rent or a percentage rent of at least 8.5 percent of your sales. How much money you make depends on many things, including the location and its popularity, the efficiency of your operating costs, and your ability to manage and control the business. Think of franchising as paying someone for his or her business strategy, marketing strategy, operations strategy, and the use of his or her name. That is pretty much what franchising is: you are establishing a relationship with a successful business so you can use its systems and capitalize on its existing brand awareness in order to get a quicker return on your own investment. You are using its proven system and name, and running it by *its* rules.

Are you still your own boss? In some respects, no. You still have to answer to someone else and follow his or her direction. You do not really own the business; you own the assets you have purchased in order to establish the business.

Unfortunately, over the years some brands have become so popular that it is hard to even get a crack at a franchise. And get this, in today's world, the franchisee with one single unit, in any industry, usually does not make enough in margins to qualify for a nice yearly income. I have known hundreds of franchisee's who feel like they own their own business, but have no freedom and are making $40,000 to $50,000 a year, after expenses, while working 60–80 hours a week!

I always say, want to buy yourself a job? Buy an existing small business or a franchise. You have effectively just bought yourself a job, and are still in the 'S' Quadrant with transactional income!

Work From Home

There are a million reasons to want to work from home. Maybe you have just had a baby and are reluctant to leave your new responsibilities. Perhaps you have been a victim of the recession and are done riding the unreliable rollercoaster of employer-based work. Or maybe you are just sick and tired of the nine-to-five grind and ready to do something you really love on your own terms. Whatever the reasons prompting your work-from-home daydreams, you should really have a plan before venturing out on your own work-from-home venture. In this book, we have got a separate chapter for work-from-home as an Independent Contractor in Network Marketing. This section is more about companies enlisting you to work for them from home, like medical transcription, or providing a service in the community that you can do from home.

With the ups and downs of the economy, the slicing of employer benefits, and the frantic pace of life, many people are starting to turn their attention towards working from home. Being able to generate an income while still maintaining control over one's life is no longer just an ideal, it is totally possible, but a fitting home business idea is the key. If you are having a hard time generating your own ideas, check out this list of home business ideas.

- Antique Appraiser
- Catering Services
- Computer Tutor
- Disc Jockey (DJ)
- EBay trader
- Gourmet Pet Food Services
- House Sitting
- House Cleaning
- Licensed Day Care Center
- Massage Therapist Home Business
- Nanny Service
- Personal Chef
- Personal Shopper and Errand Service
- Personal Trainer
- Pet Sitting
- Resume Writing Services
- Wedding Photographer
- Wedding Planner
- Homemade Baked Goods
- Wine Consultant
- Freelance Writer
- Window Cleaning

Remember, with any of these types of service businesses, it creates transactional income, which does not show up if you do not show up! It is also all about being a good networker and being able to use word-of-mouth or referral-based ideologies to successfully build your business.

Realtors can be classified here also, even though they most likely have a broker's office from which to work. I have found realtors are especially susceptible to some stinkin' thinkin' when it comes to what they actually earn, meaning the transactional basis of their earnings. I have many realtor friends who work like crazy—and I mean crazy, crazy hours, seven days a week—for the "chase" of closing a three percent deal on a $250,000 home; that is a nice $7,500 commission but after broker fees, advertising fees and taxes, it become much less. It is the chance of the big commission checks that make it addicting for realtors, but there is just no residual there, so they must do a good job saving when they do sell a home or two, and have an existing and new client list that supplies them regularly.

And then there are the numerous companies out there that are willing to "hire" you to work the phones, enter billing online, and an assortment of other responsibilities, right from your home usually as an Independent Contractor. Advancements in technology have allowed companies to even be able to track exactly what you are doing, all the time; they can track key strokes on your computer. I recently meet with a young woman who took on one of these medical transcription companies and, after four months of working with this company, was distraught with the fact that she felt completely like a slave in her own home. They knew almost exactly what she was doing all the time, therefore she always felt like she had to be "on," which was not a very pleasant experience. And again, it is all transactional income.

There are also numerous scams in the work-from-home arena. If you find a company that asks for you to send them money before they can tell you anything about the business, or to get started, walk away; 99.99 percent of the times it is a scam.

Over the years, I have spoken to hundreds who have tried one of these so-called home businesses, many with terrible experiences, so be very diligent in your analysis of any company offering you to work from home and be able to live the life of your dreams!

We have all heard the get-rich-quick claims. You know the ones. People who were supposedly down and out until they stumbled upon the secret formula for success and bam! Presto! They now have this perfect storybook life earning millions of dollars while they sleep or vacation. Right? Right! Most of these stories are with Network Marketing companies and we are going to cover them in the next chapter. What I would like to impress upon you here is what to look for when thinking about working from home.

Consider the old saying: "If it sounds too good to be true it probably is." That does not mean that every opportunity out there is a scheme or a scam nor does it mean that you cannot find a legitimate way to work from home and earn the kind of income that would allow you to pursue some of life's passions.

Network Marketing

Network Marketing comes in all kinds of packages with all kinds of names. You will hear it called a "business opportunity," "multi-level marketing" ("MLM"), "Network Marketing," "Work-from-Home," "Referral Marketing," "Relationship Marketing," "Direct Sales," "Consumer Marketing," and so on.

The Connection Economy which, as stated earlier, has been in the making for over a decade now, is a perfect fit for the Network Marketing type of Business Model. Various individuals, such as Donald Trump, Robert Kiyosaki, Mark Victor Hansen, and Paul Zane Pilzer, have written about Network Marketing as an "up and comer." I certainly believe this also.

However, if there is one thing to get out of this book, it is that not all Network Marketing companies are the same. Some, for example, have mastered the Network Marketing concept to the point of becoming the giant of their industry. Keller Williams Realty is a great example of this. Keller Williams, by 2013 now the largest real estate company in North America, operates as a Network Marketing company. Did you know that?

There is an old saying that bad news travels fast and so it goes with some of the inauthentic Network Marketing companies we will discuss here. Some of the bad ones have spoiled it for the rest. So many think anything that looks like a duck, and quacks like a duck, is a duck. Yes, there are plenty of ducks, but there are also some swans. It is the swans that you want to know about, it is the swans who have done it right, the swans will be hugely successful in the Connection Economy, like Keller Williams Realty with their profit sharing model.

I find it important to dissect the differences between the different types of compensation models that come about with all the Network Marketing companies. In my experience over the years, and with the failures that I have had along the way, I consider myself fairly well experienced in being able to dissect all the different types of models and compensation plans. Once you are around for a while, you can assess them very easily, just based upon a few key points that we have already talked about.

Network Marketing is a Business Model. It is a proven way to create a distribution system of products and services via word-of-mouth or referral marketing. Network Marketing companies operate in various industries, such as the mobile phone industry, the skin care and cosmetic industry, the weight loss industry, the travel industry, the consumer products industry, the insurance industry, the health and wellness industry, and many more.

There are three distinct compensation systems within Network Marketing companies: MLM, Direct Sales and Revenue Share/Profit Share. For example, Avon is a Network Marketing company in the skin care and cosmetic industry with a Direct Sales commission structure; Keller Williams is a Network Marketing company in the real estate industry with a revenue share/profit share commission structure; Amway is a Network Marketing company in the consumer goods industry with a MLM commission structure.

Unfortunately, the terms "Network Marketing" and "Multi-Level Marketing" are used interchangeably, even though they have very different meanings. Wikipedia uses them interchangeably, but that is not a surprise since Wikipedia is an open source encyclopedia, anyone can add their thoughts or reasoning there. It does say this at Wikipedia: "Direct selling and network marketing refer to the distribution system, while the term 'multi-level marketing' describes the compensation plan." Multi-Level Marketing (MLM) is a way of being compensated based upon multiple levels of distribution and commission on the volume of business you and your group generate, whereas the true definition of

Network Marketing is a system of creating a database or book of business on sales generated by you and others in your database. There really is a distinct difference between the definition of a MLM compensation plan and Network Marketing. Network Marketing is based upon a proven method of creating a distribution system: referral based, word-of-mouth marketing.

There are many types of industries who utilize similar ways of compensating to build their sales force and system. In the past, most insurance companies trained independent agents who would then open an office and train subagents to sell insurance policies. The agent selling the policy, the broker agent, the independent office owner, and the parent company, each would earn a commission on the ongoing policies, for as long as the policy was being serviced. This is a way of building a book of business via a commission structure of Independent Contractors; and it created a residual-style income, too. Unfortunately, that model for insurance agents has been changing over the years with the advent of the Internet insurance companies, part of this new Connection Economy—who rely on the Internet and advertising without a real independent agent relationship.

Another example of this type of compensation is your local car dealership. Ever think about the fact that car dealerships and, say, television networks, are just that: a network of independent agents or owners aligned with a parent but are building and supporting their own business utilizing a sales force and sales team and building a revenue stream that they control. That is why they are called "television networks" and "automotive networks."

Look at an example, using the car dealership. If you went and bought a car, the person who took you on the test drive, told you all about the benefits of the car, and so on, would earn a commission when you purchased the car. In fact, the car salesman would earn the largest commission, since he or she did most of the work, and made the sale. There are, however, others within the dealership who would earn a little commission off of the sale of the car that you purchased. The general manger would receive some commission, the finance manager—even if you paid cash for the car—and the parts and service manager, just to name a few. You see, in many, industries, especially if there is a sale of some commodity item—cars, insurance, consumer goods, appliances, and so on—there is an incentive for everyone to work together as a team and create sales, to get as many folks onto the lot, into the store, or in front of, to build a book of business. The only difference with all these industries is what happens *after* the sale; some are purely transactional, like cars and others, like insurance, can be residual.

The other difference is the way certain industries gather their customers, some rely strictly upon the very expensive, but tried and true, advertising forum of television, radio, print and billboard, while Network Marketing companies rely solely on their Independent Contractors to be customer gatherers.

So, over the years, Network Marketing has evolved as one which is based upon the Independent Contractors building a book of business, earning a commission from those in their database, without the parent company, the actual owner of the product or service, doing any traditional advertising; it is all on the backs of the Independent Contractor to gather potential customers.

According to About.com:

> *Network Marketing is just a business model, and it really amounts to 'micro-franchising.' Its upside is that it has a very low cost of entry, with the potential for exceptional revenue, and there are those who achieve that.*
>
> *But those same things that make it attractive make it attractive to many who are NOT really qualified or prepared to become business owners…Network Marketing is a great opportunity for people to have their first business, their first sales role, etc. My point is this—recognize it for what it is: it's a business, and you are a business owner. And if you've never owned a business before, if you've never done sales before, if you've never networked before, you need to learn about how to do so, not just from the network marketing experts, but from established experts in those fields.*
>
> *Network Marketers who are serious about building a business should be reading and learning about business fundamentals, the latest sales and marketing techniques, strategies for networking and business development, etc., not just swapping tips at your team's weekly or monthly meeting. Act like a small business owner, and people will treat you like one.*

So, it is just like everything we have been discussing in this book: if you are going to be entrepreneurial, regardless of the idea or model, then just go into it with a good amount of education and knowledge. If you do not want to be your own boss, with all that comes with it, then you may be better off working for someone else, punching the clock, and having the potential security of a weekly check and benefits. Entrepreneurship certainly does not fit everyone!

If Network Marketing is your way to go, look for a great new resource book on the new economy and how Network Marketing fits, as well as how to be a Network Marketing Professional, called *Go Pro, 7 Steps To Becoming A Network Marketing Professional* by Eric Worre, a 30-year-veteran of Network Marketing. It has some of the best insights I have seen in understanding the Network Marketing Model, and how to be a successful entrepreneur by becoming a Network Marketing Professional.

Chapter 11

Is It A Duck?

"When looking over a lake you see lots of ducks, but the swans are the real attraction."

– Harvey Hess

I am sure you have heard the old saying that if it walks like a duck, and quacks like a duck, then it must be a duck. I get it. So, we will see if we can find out what makes the duck, and why it is the swans that you are looking for in Network Marketing; they do not walk or quack like a duck, but many times get lumped in with all the ducks.

Many of the stories you hear about the Network Marketing Profession these days have been passed down, decade-to-decade, generation-to-generation. It is a profession that has certainly had growing pains, like many other professions in becoming legitimized, and, thus, the stories sometimes get larger as time goes on. As an example, in the late 60s and early 70s my mother, while raising six children, decided she was going to help with the family finances. Someone had introduced her to a party plan company selling skin care utilizing mink oil. All I remember about that experience is all these products around the house and faux leather carrying kits of skin care and oil all about the house. That experience did not turn out well for my mother, but she still lives today to tell the story of that failed experience and the huge amount of inventory in mink oil products we had around the house for years to come.

I doubt that my mother received any kind of training and she was most likely not getting much support; there was not any system to plug into and, as it pertains to Network Marketing, she was an amateur who gave up fairly quickly. Even though my parents have been one of my customers of the Network Marketing Company I represent for 11 years now, she and my father grimaced when I told them I was going to be a Network Marketing Professional for the rest of my life. Their story is not unlike many others through the 60s, 70s, 80s and 90s; 40–50 years of stories, some really good, most not so good. It has been a profession and a model growing up for 50 years now.

I was reading Pamela Slim's excellent work, *Escape from Cubicle Nation: From Corporate Prisoner to Thriving Entrepreneur*, when I came across a few pages in which she warns her readers about leaving a job to be involved in Network Marketing. I was at first disappointed, since it was, in my opinion, throwing all the swans in with the ducks, but completely understand the rationale at work:

> *Of all the business models that scare people, multilevel marketing (MLM) or network marketing has to top the list. Many, many people have reservations about participating in this business model, which often promises huge profits for very little work.*
>
> *For those of you who work in multilevel marketing and have always been ethical, what I am about to say may make you angry. I truly do not mean to offend or present an exceptionally lopsided analysis, I just want to share some words of warning to overeager entrepreneurs who might get themselves into something that will not feel good at the best, and may affect family and friend relationships at the worst.*
>
> *Here is an example from a longtime blog reader who was kind enough to share his own personal story about living with a parent who got involved with Amway:*
>
> *"My father was a creative, intelligent, hardworking man with an entrepreneurial dream. When I was ten, his union struck the shipyard where he had worked for seventeen years. He was out of a job as the strike continued indefinitely until his job was replaced. He found work as a welder in a paper mill and built a stump-grinding machine that he used on the weekend to make extra money. Eventually, he became reemployed in the shipbuilding industry, but always 's a contract employee.*
>
> *A coworker introduced him to Amway. It was much more than a business opportunity; it was a chance to realize our family's dream of financial freedom. For Amway we made lists...lists of all our friends and acquaintances that my mom was to call and invite over*

to our house. We were under strict instructions not to tell them it was Amway. She couldn't do it—it was humiliating and dishonest. My dad retired to his study to read endless motivational books and listen to tapes (purchased from our upline sponsor) full of people talking about their successes. He was inspired, but translating theory into practice eluded us.

We attended many meetings—my dad tape recorded many of them for later study. The meeting were a never ending parade of people who had made their $50,000/year, quit their jobs, and bought expensive cars and jewelry. It was the 1980s and these people were living a materialist dream—while underneath them, hundreds, like my parents, struggled to change their mindset, to "think and grow rich", to believe in the 'magic of thinking big.'

As a child, I was aware of the conflict this created between my parents but I did not fully understand the costs. It was an exciting sort of game and the books were inspiring. I wanted my dad to succeed. But the business is fundamentally based on using your personal connections not only to sell a product, but to enlist those you know into a get-rich scheme where compromising your values (using people) is a fundamental prerequisite to success. It has affected my view of the world to this day—I am deeply suspicious of personal networking and have a distrust of wealth. My father's obsession with MLMs destroyed his marriage (my parents divorced during my freshman year away at college) and left him a lonely man who died alone at sixty-three with years of accumulated motivational books and tapes that I was left to literally shovel in the trash as I cleaned his house to attempt to sell it to cover his medical bills."

It is stories like these, and many factors that are less prominent now than in the past, which have created these tales about the Network Marketing Profession, especially if you are over 40 years old. I have a few myself from just 12 or 14 years ago.

Most of the issues that had created the stories have been cleaned out, cleaned up and eradicated. It is still a process, however, and there still are some ducks that need to be recognized. Partnering with the right company, one that fits your beliefs, passion and desires, is first and foremost. Secondly, you must be ready to work, better be ready to be coachable, to learn new skills, to be a business owner. Anyone starting a

Network Marketing business must have thick skin, or as Network Marketing Professional Eric Worre states in his book, 'Go Pro' "You must accept a temporary loss of social esteem from ignorant people." If you cannot handle that statement, then entrepreneurship may not be in your best interest. It is what it is, as they say.

So, how do you identify the correct company?

There are three very important factors to consider with any company you may be investigating, and one very important factor about you. The three company facts are company management, the Law of Consumerism, which we have outlined previously, and the amount of hype being presented by the current lot of Independent Contractors. The you factor is all about your seriousness in becoming a Network Marketing Professional, for example, treating the business like a real business, doing what is necessary, not as a poser or amateur.

In order to truly understand the different models and compensation plans with all Direct Sales companies, you must first understand some of the basics behind the terminology, the compensation systems, and the Business Models.

As I mentioned in the previous chapter, there are three distinct compensation systems within Network Marketing companies: **MLM, Direct Sales, and Revenue Share/Profit Share.** We will take a look at each.

Direct Sales / Retail Sales

There are many companies, such as Avon, Mary Kay, Arbonne, Scentsy Candles, CAbi Clothes and Pampered Chief who operate as a Direct Sales/Distributor-Based Business Model, occasionally known as "party plan." They do not operate as a MLM commission structure; it is a retail sales commission structure. Anyone becoming a distributor with these companies becomes an independent distributor who must purchase inventory, at wholesale rates, catalogs, and sales tools; must take all the orders, handle all the money from sales, place all the orders with the company; and must handle all returns, and, heaven forbid, handle any bad checks, credit cards, or charge backs. The money earned by these distributors is the difference between the wholesale price they pay and retail price that the customer pays.

Many of the top Networking Companies have done a phenomenal job with this type of Direct Sales model. Being an ex-retailer, I can certainly tell you that the amount of money saved in overhead, physical locations, employees, and so on allows the Direct Sales model to put forth a profitable business. That is why, I am certain, that one of the most astute businessmen in the U.S.A., Warren Buffet, bought the majority stake of Pampered Chef in 2002.

In some cases, distributors of Direct Sales companies are compensated to help others also become distributors, until the point that the new distributor's business is at par or above with their monthly volume; then they "break away" on their own, or the compensated "manager" receives a very small commission on the ongoing sales of that particular leg. That is not much of an incentive to really help others succeed though! Generally , those with a break away as part of their compensation plan is a flaw, since it just does not really give anyone an incentive to step up and be a leader.

The 'burn out' rate, or attrition, from these types of businesses can be quite high. As an example, the average Avon distributor works their business for six months. On the other hand, they all do an incredible job building "community" and being part of the mission of that company. Mary Kay Cosmetics has probably been best in class with their distributors being emotionally all in with the Mary Kay Company and very committed to the mission of helping women be independent business owners.

There are literally thousands of Direct Sales, party plan companies in North America, and more popping up all the time. It has become a very low cost of entry model for owners with a product or service idea. Just like any industry though, the success rate can be quite low, with hundreds of companies here one year, gone the next—or barely holding on. Apply the factors we discussed in the last chapter if you are looking at a Direct Sales company and remember this other very important factor: it is purely transactional income, it does not really get you to the 'B' Quadrant but places you squarely in the 'S' Quadrant.

The majority of Direct Sales companies are swans; there are not many, if any, ducks here.

MLM compensation plan

Just about all of the criticism and consternation with the Network Marketing profession can be directly tied to this way of compensation. This is where many of the ducks have resided over the years. It certainly does not mean that a Network Marketing company with a MLM compensation structure is not viable and authentic; many are really good companies that are well-operated, have a great history, and have been a blessing for many, physically and financially. Unfortunately, though, many of the stories and past experiences of distributors being "garage qualified," or having to stick products in the garage, of losing hundreds, and often thousands of dollars, of overhyped statements of potential earnings, and of failed Network Marketing companies, of which there are thousands, just about all stem from the flaws in this particular way of compensation. You must be good at recognizing the red flags.

MLM is Network Marketing with a compensation system of multiple levels of distribution that rewards those with higher commissions who have built a larger volume of business. MLM compensation systems come in all kinds of sizes and shapes, from the unilevel plan and binaries, from Australian 2-ups to matrix, hybrid unilevels/binaries, and so on. They can be well disguised! Usually, the commissions paid are higher if that person's group volume (GV), the size and purchases of their organization, is larger than the person below them, and below them, and so on. That is why MLM actually means being paid increasing commission percentages on levels of distribution, depending upon the size of your organization. One of the obvious problems with this way of compensation is that if you are one of the lucky ones, the top 2 to 5 percent, who got in early, then you earn the largest commissions. As a newbie, you are told that you can earn the "big money" when you advance to those levels but the majority are never able to advance because of the flaws in the model, and then quit.

Unfortunately, many of these companies have, or had, really good marketing, really good spin, that makes it seem like if you begin today, and invite a few others to do the same, in a short amount of time dump trucks full of money are going to show up at your house. You will be wealthy. And that is the furthest from the truth. It is work, and it is hard work. Building a lifelong residual income takes more than just a few people. Red flag.

And a few more red flags:

- *The need for the product or service*: many times the product or service is something that is not currently being utilized by the average consumer, it is a new need developed and new money being spent. Also, the way they must price the product or services to provide the money for the compensation plan, much of which is "promotional volume," which will be discussed more coming up. Red flag.
- *Commission status*: Must you spend more than a typical monthly need of the particular product or service in order to be paid a commission? Many times in analyzing a company, I can guess at how much the distributor, or business owner, associate, or whatever term is used, has to purchase monthly in personal volume since it has to fit the compensation model. Try it yourself, and you will see that the usual amount of personal volume required for product companies is almost always somewhere between $120–$240 per month, and it is typically more than can be consumed, in a month. The NMMLM company usually wants you to retail the extra product, or give it away as samples. For phone, travel, and other service oriented companies, the start-up costs, which is the money to fund the compensation plan, are higher, and the monthly requirement normally has to do with the conversion to their service plus a website cost of between $50–$100 a month. This could be a red flag, depending upon the actual need and price.
- *"Ground Floor!"*: I have heard that one so many times it is amazing. When a company touts the fact that you must get in early, secure your place, your position, before others so you can "be in the money," red flag. I have often wondered what they will do in a year or two when it is no longer "ground floor." What becomes the next pitch? Rather short-sighted, right?
- *Company management/ownership*: Are the owners some Network Marketers who thought they could do it better than the company they were representing, so started their own, even though they have no real business experience at a corporate

level? Are there a bunch of family members involved? Do the owners/management have positions in the compensation plan? Red flags.

- *We pay out over 60 percent*: Or some other number which is totally ridiculous. If a Network Marketing company is paying out more than 40 percent in commissions then something is amiss, either the company is running on a shoestring, the products are being manufactured in some underground factory overseas, or the price is so sky high, there is no long-term business potential. Red flag.
- *Gimmicks*: If the company allows, or offers, multiple positions in the business, if they allow a person to buy excess inventory, if they allow you to know exactly what your volume is monthly, then "buy-up" in order to earn an additional commission, bonus or status advancement. Red flag.

NMMLM companies get scrutinized often, and because of the flaws in the compensation system, they have hurt many people over the years. I have unfortunately even succumbed to the hype. I received quite a costly education at the hands of an ex-pastor who had made a lot of money with a now defunct NMMLM selling diet cookies. He then went on to start his own NMMLM company and was a master at telling the story, getting people emotionally drawn in, and preaching promises of big money to be made. Looking back now, there were so many red flags that I am even embarrassed to say that I got sucked in. That experience did not turn out very well as that ex-company owner has now been jailed for 30 years for U.S. securities fraud. It is so sad to say but in many ways he deserved all that he has now received.

Many times however, NMMLM companies have a solid product, sometimes even backed up by clinical trials and good science and research. The products are usually manufactured by a third-party manufacturing facility, but the normal retail and/or wholesale price of the product or service does not match the price of similar products in the grocery stores; it just has to fit the compensation plan. I mentioned that old saying earlier that "if you want to dine with the classes then you must deal with the masses."

It really does not matter how much a company hypes its juice, or other elixir, essential oil, skin cream, or newfangled phone; if you cannot take that product to a Wal*Mart store, place it on the shelf with other similar products in that category, and it fit right in, price, value, trust, and convenience—the Law of Consumerism—then you have a product that is reliant on someone buying it only with the hope of making money, not because they really want it, use it, and need it. When you extract the product from the money-making opportunity, the simple question is, would you still buy that product, at that price, and use it consistently? Would you ask your mother to buy the product also? And believe me, I am not saying that there are not good products out there in the NMMLM marketplace. I have been a customer for decades of various products that are of high quality, and fit my needs at the time, I was just willing to pay a higher price for the product than what would be deemed normal.

As example, back in 1985 I was introduced to a product called KM, a potassium mineral supplement; its claim to fame was that its discovery happened by a doctor, who, when climbing the Alps in his native Austria, was faint of oxygen and so went looking for the solution, via botanicals, that would help his blood oxygenate. The story was impressive, and was the centerpiece of the company. Years later it was discovered that the story was fiction. You have to have a story, many times, with an overpriced NMMLM product. Back then, I was becoming interested in residual-style income since the leading distributors were a couple and their sons and daughters, who I came to know, and they were really making it big. I received a few bottles via automatic shipments each and every month and became emotionally tied to the product. After figuring out that I was not very good at getting others to buy the stuff, I just continued to be a customer, receiving my couple of bottles every month, costing me around $120 a month and went along receiving it for literally 15 years! It was not until the company sold off the rest of what they had—they first entered Bankruptcy in 1995—that I finally stopped receiving my monthly bottles of KM. I became hooked, emotionally, to the product, not ever really knowing if it was all that good for me, but my logic was that it could not hurt!

The problem comes when you try to get others to spend the $30–40 a bottle for a juice product that is not normally in their budget. In the category of juices, for example, the masses that are buying any type of

Juice product, think Welsh's Grape Juice, do so in the $5 range. So, if you are trying to sell a juice in the $30–40 range, what might be the size of your market? The size is really only those who are thinking, or trying, to make money themselves; or those, like myself, who simply get emotionally hooked to the product. Worse yet for those companies is the fact that if a traditional chain store, like Costco, gets pitched on the new juice phenomenon made with these special berries from Asia or South America, you will now see knock-offs of the juice product for 50 percent, 60 percent even 80 percent less than the one being touted by the NMMLM company. It is then that they really have to go all out on marketing and storytelling to convince you that their particular product is different. The Law of Consumerism at work: price, trust, value, and convenience. And that is the rest of the story!

But I have one even better about another NMMLM experience I had. This one is even comical! It was 2002 and I had just left the company with the pastor now in jail—that was a one-year disaster for me personally—only to meet some great guys there that all decided to start their own NMMLM company (red flag!). It was to be called The TopLine. And the product? Well, it was a winner: cell phones. Everything was in place, I was one of the Founding Members, made an initial investment in the business, which, by the way, totaled $50,000 (all the Founding Members become vested owners), and off we go! For about six months. Our supplier (red flag), WorldCom Wireless, had just landed in deep water with the U.S. Securities and Exchange Commission, filed bankruptcy, and the eventual owner of WorldCom ended up going to prison (that is another whole story and book!). We were now scrambling.

This is why I talk all the time about whether a company has control of the manufacturing and distribution process; if they have margins available in the product line, or are just a reseller of someone else's product. It is amazing to see the plethora of juice-oriented NMMLM companies out there, as an example, who have some hyped-up story about their product, and when you do the research, you find that there are only three juice manufacturers in the country—two in Utah and one in Arizona—who manufacture all of the juice products for those 60 to 70 different companies. Who has the control? Not the NMMLM company. Who controls the margins? Not the NMMLM company. Why do they have to price the product way out of where the masses are buying? To fit the MLM compensation plan.

Okay, on with the story. Once we lost our feature product—one that the now-6000 distributors wanted to be a part of—the company was scrambling to find something, anything, to fit into the compensation plan. And what did they find? A diet product! So, now we go from our story about our great cell phone program to a story about our new diet, the Amazon Diet! We had to come up with the marketing material, the story about the ingredients, from deep in the Amazon jungle that have now been discovered to help people lose weight. Are you kidding me? Wait, it gets better. I even secure a place on the local television channel to tout this new diet, and at the time I was about 40 pounds overweight myself! One of the most embarrassing moments of my life, and I still have the tape of it! Oh my. Okay, you can quit laughing now; get up off the floor!

Well, as you can imagine, that flamed out, too, leaving the company with no option but to find a buyer, but a buyer of what? The only asset now was a bunch of folks who had not made any money for a year, many had already left for the next deal they could find, so not much was left. But, believe it or not, somehow, the company was able to sell its database, the downline of distributors, to a company in the waterless car wash business. So now, here I am, one year after thinking that we had something pretty good in cell phones, especially in 2002 before the entry of the big cell phone players, to a powered diet with herbs from the Amazon that tasted horrid, to a line of waterless car wash products. Are you still laughing? Quit it!

Well, I was crying, and crying, and crying. Can you imagine now getting a box auto-shipped each month with bottles of waterless car wash? And you can guess how much the auto-ship was, right? Yep, $120. I did not know what to do! Was there any way to recover the $50,000 invested in this disaster? Nope. It was gone, I had quite a learning experience, and felt like a fool. But, for some strange reason, I did not cancel my waterless car wash auto-ship until I had a few shelves in the garage full of it. And just a few weeks ago, in a conversation with my now 27 year old son, he brought up the fact that I had tried to put he and a friend in business washing cars, with no water, in shopping center parking lots at 15 years old. I said "Yep, that was fun, wasn't it!" And he said, "Well, I still have a whole plastic container full of that stuff, I am thinking of making a few bucks on the side doing it again." I said "'Go for it, son." What else are you going to do with a 10 year supply of waterless car wash products?

Unfortunately, many more fail than succeed when a Network Marketing company has an MLM compensation system that does not meet the Law of Consumerism, and especially has some of the red flags identified here.

What I have discovered is that with any company, if your passion is not about the company mission, and belief in what they are doing, if it is not about helping others with ways to improve their lives, if it is only about you making money, if it is only about you and what this thing will do for you, then you are not being authentic, not being truthful. You are saying one thing, but thinking and doing something totally opposite. You are being a hypocrite, and many are and can sleep like babies at night. I just do not believe it should be that way.

That is just not how the Network Marketing Profession will continue to be legitimized. It will be by being authentic, no gimmicks, no games, and no hype. It will be.

So, the reason NMMLM companies sometimes get a bad name for themselves is that people overpay for products or services, with the hype that they can achieve wealth by getting others to overpay for a product or service. It just does not meet the Law of Consumerism. It is an inauthentic product or service.

These are the ones that look like a duck and quack like a duck; they really are a duck! Please, do not feed the ducks! Find the swans, you must look closely, but there are a few swans with this compensation system.

Revenue or Profit Sharing Plans

Some companies, such as Keller Williams in the real estate industry, operate with a different model. Yes, they are Network Marketing companies, but they do not have a MLM compensation system; they offer profit sharing or revenue sharing. These are the swans of the business also and, just like when you go to a lake and see all the waterfowl, there just are not very many of them, unfortunately! The difference in this model is the method of marketing and compensation. Keller Williams, for example, pays a profit share to the agents hanging their licenses at a Keller Williams office who recruit other agents to join the team. This type of compensation is totally fair to everyone and is really no different, except maybe in the terminology, to your local car distributorship who pays the majority of the commissions on a car sale to the person who sold the car, but a share of the commission goes to the general manager, the parts and service manager and the finance manager. It is an extremely fair and equitable way to compensate. In the Keller Williams example though, due to the nature of residential real estate sales, it does not create a true, ongoing reliable residual income; it creates more of a transactional income stream and is not always reliable monthly.

There are other companies out there who rely on Independent Contractors to build a book of business but are compensated for bringing a customer to the company, while also being compensated to train, support, and mentor others to do the same. It really takes some critical analysis of the compensation system, what you are actually spending your money on, what you are being paid to provide others, whether the product or service fits the Law of Consumerism, and whether you would purchase the product or service without the advent of the business. And more importantly, would you ask your mother to do the same and be able to put your head on the pillow at night?

One of the truest ways to analyze the different types of businesses, is to do the cash flow test. What you must do is answer this question: Where does the money come from and how does the money flow? This is one of the most critical aspects of delineating the various types of Business Models and compensation systems. Does the compensation plan make money off of people or does it "recover" money that would normally be allocated as an expense? If the business is promotionally-driven, meaning that the majority of sales come from the front-loading of inventory' from the back-loading through having to buy more than you can use monthly; in spending new money on fad-type products you have lived without all your life to this point; in the "topping up" to achieve volume requirements to advance in status; or even in the payment of a sum of money for the right to ask others for the same amount of payment with no real product—then it is very easy to see that the money is not coming from the purchase of real products, by real people, because they really need them, or simple redirected spending. It is coming from the false economy of promotion. This is why the vast majority of participants with some companies are just customers, and why the vast majority of participants with the ducks quit.

The money the swans pay to those building a business does not come off the backs of others via "promotional volume," but from the distribution and advertising dollars they save, by doing things like manufacturing their own products, controlling the supply chain, or doing little to no advertising or marketing. Its customers are also a part of the process by shopping direct, eliminating the retail and wholesale stores, receiving a better price and value, and so on. It comes from the advertising dollars that are built-in to the retail price of products we buy at the store, and that are simply "redirected" to their customers if they refer other customers.

Put a different way, is it a fair and equitable system for all or does the person getting in early, or at the top, always make the majority of the income, ergo the "pyramid" concern? In some NMMLM compensation systems, there is always the ability for the person preceding you to earn more on your efforts than you, either because they were in earlier, they have higher "group volume" so they make higher bonuses, or they have "balanced legs," as used in a binary compensation plan, etc.

A few Network Marketing companies without MLM compensation systems operate like the tried and proven compensation systems of other respected industries like real estate, insurance or auto sales. The person who brings in the business always makes the majority of the commission, but there is a team that earns an equal or smaller commission to support, train and encourage others. Bring in a new customer and you earn the majority of the commission, not those above you. You earn the residual on your personal customers, those in your support team only earn a smaller amount for mentoring, coaching, supporting. This is structured exactly like the industries mentioned earlier.

Follow where the money comes from and how it flows and you will have either an authentic business or an inauthentic business!

So, when looking at Network Marketing companies that have a Direct Sales compensation system, an MLM compensation system, or a Revenue Share/Profit Share compensation system, here are 8 logical factors that I discovered are key to identify and separate an honest and legitimate business concept from all the others.

You must have a real product that customers will really want and need versus the latest overprice fad product or over-hyped product.

For example, as I just discussed earlier, there are a lot of Network Marketing businesses these days selling miracle fruit juices that supposedly heal everything that ails you! How many people do you know that would willingly spend $35–$40 a bottle on fruit juice? And if these juices really do hold all the miracle claims they purportedly do, Welch's and other billion dollar company giants would be selling them for $3 a bottle versus $35 in no time. It is already happening. Take a look next time you are in Costco and you will see dozens of these exotic juices for sale at a fraction of the price. People might pay twice as much for a product if it can be proven to be better quality than the cheaper version but probably not five or ten times as much. Overpriced, exotic products with wild claims are usually a red flag for a business of questionable legitimacy. They are inauthentic. Stay away.

Are there reasonable start-up costs and do you get value for your money invested?

Run from any business that asks you to send them money before they will even give you the details of what their business is all about. Also view opportunities that have large inventory requirements with a great deal of skepticism as well. In today's modern marketplace with direct fulfillment ability, which means you can have products shipped direct to your customer, why would you need to make a large investment of thousands of dollars? Those types of companies are in the business of selling inventory to suckers versus selling real products to customers. You probably should avoid those deals. There is no need for you to have to stock products, take orders, or make deliveries. A good Business Model will take care of these things on your behalf.

Does the company behind the products have a money-back guarantee?

This is straightforward. Anything less than a 30-day unconditional money back guarantee is highly suspect, and may actually even be illegal in some jurisdictions. Good companies will even take back used products for a refund, although it would be entirely understandable if they charged a small restocking fee for this. Many companies are notorious for changing product labels or packaging in order to render product "obsolete" in order to avoid having to give refunds, even if they state they offer a refund. So make sure you read the fine print before you get stuck with something.

What exactly do you get paid for doing?

Most people know it is illegal almost everywhere for you to get paid solely on the act of recruiting a new participant into a money-making opportunity. You can only be paid when an actual product or service of value is moved to an end-user. There are a lot of companies, especially those with MLM compensation systems that walk a fine line with this one. For example, there are several telecom or technology based companies that charge you $500 to become a Marketing Representative, which really buys you nothing more than the ability to earn commissions when you recruit other reps. They may have had their legal team cleverly disguise this payment for the act of recruiting as bonuses you earn when you help others recruit, but the question is, what does the $500 actually buy you? Is there any product of real value changing hands here? A closer look usually reveals that most of the commissions being paid in those businesses is being generated from the $500 people are paying to get started and not the movement of a real product or service to the end user. Money just changing hands. Inauthentic.

Does the company have a track record?

Every company claims they are successful but can it be verified though independent sources? Check the Better Business Bureau in their home state or province. Do they have a Dunn and Bradstreet number and rating? How long have they been in business? Are they debt-free? Do they have total quality control of and manufacture their own products? Have they ever been featured in legitimate business publications like *Inc.* Magazine? Do not be fooled by companies featured in magazines like *Success*, *Entrepreneur* or *Home-Based Business*, as most of these publications will actually sell their cover page or feature story to any company that wants to pay for it. You cannot buy your way onto the Inc. 500 list or Fortune 500 list. Make sure companies are not paying for someone to herald them. It is much more credible when this comes from independent sources.

What kind of training and support is offered?

One of the biggest reasons that franchising has been such a successful Business Model is because the person purchasing the franchise from the master franchisor is buying a proven system of success. I would suggest you apply this same reasoning to any Network Marketing business you might be considering. Are the people you will be teaming up with already successful? What is their track record? Do they have the blueprint and resources for you to easily duplicate that are provided for a very reasonable or even no cost at all? Stay clear of companies that end up expecting you to invest hundreds of dollars a month for their "systems." It is a sure sign they are making money off the system versus from helping you be successful.

Avoid any businesses that claim they will build it all for you.

Nothing should make you laugh more than the advertisements offering to build your business for you. The reason is simple: Why do they need you if they are going to build it all for you? Why not just build it all for themselves? The answer is simple: they do not need you, they just want your money! People who want something for nothing still get sucked into this offer. And while they may not have to do much, they will always end up paying a lot, usually with little or no results.

Find a product that replaces something people are already buying but offers better value and convenience.

The old saying that you can make a lot of money if you build a better mousetrap is still true today. A great example in recent history of this is the video rental company Netflix. Before they burst on to the scene, no one could compete with Blockbuster's buying power. This ensured they always had dozens of copies of the latest releases at reasonable prices and they had a store in every neighborhood to make it convenient for the customer. But they still had huge overhead with thousands of stores. Netflix came along and made a better mousetrap. Without the overhead of thousands of stores, Netflix could afford to mail videos directly to your home making it cost effective and even more convenient than your local Blockbuster video. The product was the same, but the Business Model was disruptive. So Netflix captured a huge market share almost overnight of a product people were already spending money on. Make sense?

A legitimate business will offer this kind of value and convenience to the customer. So find something they already spend money on, improve the quality and convenience, and you will have a hit that can create long-term sustainable income.

So, when looking at any potential company for you to align with, take the eight items above and get the answer before making a decision.

A Word About Word-of-Mouth Marketing (WOMM)

I have been amazed over the past 10 years with the advancement of referral or word-of-mouth marketing. The advancements have been astronomical and, with the continuing advancement of social media, I believe that person-to-person marketing is really just getting started.

Referral marketing, or word-of-mouth marketing, is one of the fastest growing ways to market in North America and beyond today. Over the years, as advertising has seen a decrease in effectiveness, WOMM has seen such an increase that there is now an association: the Word-of-Mouth Marketing Association (www.womma.org). This organization is targeted towards traditional businesses wanting to increase their exposure, utilizing WOMM. Other companies, such as BzzAgent (www.bzzagent.com) started over the past 10 years to utilize WOMM and social marketing to "Buzz" a company's product and or service. These traditional ways of trying to utilize WOMM always miss one key ingredient: Being compensated for your efforts, and not just one time via a free product or service, but over and over again for the delivery of a customer, as long as the customer continues to be a customer.

I was one of the very first BzzAgents back in 2002, and still am today. Over the years, I have received numerous products and services, along with a media packet, coupons, and other marketing tools, to buzz about the product. There is always instructions on how to buzz—interesting! I found that when I received something that really gravitated with me, like a Logitech universal remote control that made my life in the living room simpler, I talked about it endlessly. But when I received a product that did not really enhance my life, I just could not talk about it. You will always tell your friends and relatives about a good movie, restaurant or other product or service that enhanced your life, but it has to be genuine and something that you have a little passion behind.

That is the reason Network Marketing is growing faster as a Business Model than any other marketing approach today. According to the Direct Selling Association (www.dsa.org), in 2013, the most recent figures available, over $32 billion in sales occurred via Network Marketing in the U.S.A., an almost five percent increase in sales over the previous year, and that is in the midst of a fairly poor economic climate. There is more and more acceptance in the marketplace of the legitimacy of well-run, proven Network Marketing companies.

Another analogy on the ongoing acceptance of Network Marketing would be to look at the history of franchising. In the late 50s/early 60s, the franchise Business Model was under extreme pressure for being an illegal model. Franchising came within a few votes in Congress of being outlawed as a way to market. It was felt that the franchisee and the customers would be unfairly treated if a company could "sell" their system, then hold each owner under contract to do it exactly the same way. Do you think that over time franchising was readily accepted by the masses and today is a proven Business Model? Absolutely. The same will go for well-run, above-board, authentic Network Marketing companies, like Keller Williams Realty, who announced this past year that they are now the largest real estate brand in North America.

WOMM Case Study: Do you have a Costco card? Do you know someone who does? Someone who shops at Costco? Do you know that Costco created a $90 billion a year Business Model and never, not once, did they utilize traditional forms of advertising to build their business? Have you ever seen a Costco commercial? Never. Costco created an enormous company, all on WOMM. Just think about when you discovered Costco, did you tell anyone about it? So many of us did, and it just kept spreading and spreading that everyone either knows of or shops at Costco today, without the company ever spending a dime on advertising, just selling memberships. Amazing.

What do you think your life would look like today if, when Costco came to your neighborhood, they said, "Every time you refer a customer our way, and every time they shop at our store, we will pay you a small commission for that referral." Think about that one for a minute. That is the power of word-of-mouth Network Marketing where you are paid an ongoing commission just to switch customers to a different place to secure products and services that they need and buy regularly.

If you do your homework, your due diligence, and find a business that hits on all cylinders that we are discussing in this book, the sky, and your life, has no limits. Dream about it...

Become a Great Networker

Sometimes, just the idea of Networking makes people uncomfortable. But for you to create a lifelong, residual income, it really is all about learning the skill to be a good Networker. This new normal, the Connection Economy, is all about new skills, and one of those skills is becoming a good connector, a good communicator, and a good networker.

When most people think about networking it seems insincere at best and selfish at worst. This, of course, is the complete opposite of what networking is supposed to be: friendly, useful, and genuine. If you are passionate about the product or service you represent, if you are emotionally all in and know in your heart that you are providing a great service, or product, to others, if you know that it simply cannot hurt anyone, then it becomes easy to Network.

It is especially easy for most of us to be friendly and useful with people we know. However, because networking is a "business activity" it is also easy to think that we need to act in a different way.

Unfortunately, most networking strategies come across as pushy, needy, or self-serving—even though the people using them rarely act that way in day-to-day life.

Do not worry, there are definitely genuine ways to self-promote. Let us take a look at some ways to be a great networker.

The real goal of networking

> **The goal of networking should be to help other people.** Yes, it would be nice if they helped you out as well, but networking is a two-way street. And your side of the street is all about helping others, not asking them to help you. Asking for favors should only become a possibility once you have learned more about the person and provided some value to them.
>
> **It is far more important to understand their needs before you tell them about your needs.** Your goals should not be on

the forefront of your mind. You are trying to develop a relationship with someone, which means you should be thinking about them. It is your job to understand the people in your network, where they are coming from, and what is important to them.

Setting expectations

You do not need to know the most people, just the right people. There is no need to shotgun your business cards across the industry or to pepper everyone with emails. Instead, focus on finding people that are relevant to you. As time goes on, you can decide if the interests that you share with someone are worth pursuing further. It is better to have five people willing to help you out than it is to have 500 that simply know your name.

Do not expect anything. The fact that you reached out and made contact with someone does not put them in your debt. No one is required to "pay you back." Instead of approaching networking with the goal of gaining favors, try reaching out with curiosity. Contact interesting and relevant people and see what happens. Some of them will respond and some of them will not. Learn about the people that follow up. Find out what makes them interesting and how you can help them—and do not expect anything in return.

Do not leave networking to chance. Take some time and define what you are looking for in your network. Every once and awhile you will stumble across someone amazing on accident, but it is a lot easier to find who you are looking for if you know who they are in the first place. Be proactive and create a list of people that you want to contact on purpose.

Go beyond your industry. Connect with people on a variety of levels from a wide range of areas. By growing your network outside of the usual areas you will be more valuable to people that are in your immediate industry. The people you work with have personalities and multiple interests, right? With a broad network you can be the person that connects people across industries.

Do not dismiss anyone as irrelevant. There is an old saying that, on average, 200 people show up at a funeral. That would mean that on average, every person's circle of influence is around 200 people. No one is irrelevant; they can lead you to someone, almost all the time.

How to reach out to someone new

Quantify how much time you are going to take. People are busy and when someone new starts talking to them, the first thing that comes to their mind is "How long is this person going to talk to me?" or "How much time is this going to take?"

Address those concerns from the start by saying something like, "Hi. I have one item that I would like to briefly discuss with you. It should only take two minutes. Do you have time now?" Asking questions like this not only show that you respect their time, it also gives you the option of speaking with them later if they are too busy now.

Start by offering praise, not requesting help. Unless you have a mutual contact that is putting you in touch for a specific reason, it is best to avoid asking for anything when you meet for the first time. Do not ask for favors, for promotion, for advice, or even to meet up for lunch or coffee. Simply start by offering a short compliment. After they respond to this initial contact, you can begin moving things towards a lengthier meeting.

Keep your communication short. If your first contact is via email, then split the message into smaller segments. Instead of reaching out to someone new with a long-winded, five paragraph explanation of why you are contacting them, use that first email to focus on a small bit of praise. You can send further details to them after they reply. Keep that first message friendly and short. In today's world, utilizing text, Facebook, Twitter and other social media offerings is even better. Short and sweet.

How to build the relationship

Try to provide as much value as you possibly can. The more value you create, the more it will come back to you many times over. Focus all of your networking efforts on helping the people you contact.

Start by focusing on being friendly and helpful. This is the number one tactic you can use to build your network: simply spread information in a friendly and helpful way. Did you read a book that someone in your network will enjoy? (Hey, how about this one! LOL) Tell them about it or send them a copy. Are you using something that would help a friend with a project they are working on? Email it to them. Hear a new music album that someone might enjoy? Send it their way. Building your network is the same as building friends. Be interested in what they are doing and offer friendly suggestions when you can.

Develop the habit of introducing people. Connecting like-minded people is a powerful tool to enhance your network. The idea of doing this seems foreign to many people, but it is actually quite easy. Do you know two people who enjoy reading the same type of books? Or like the same sports teams? Or love reading about history? Or work in the same industry? You get the point. Do not make it hard, just introduce the two of them by sharing their common interest. They can decide if they want to pursue the relationship further.

Ask if people want to be connected. If you are apprehensive about connecting two people, then ask one of them if they want to be connected. "I know another person that is doing Y. Would you like for me to introduce you sometime?" Even if they are not interested, they will appreciate the offer.

Nurture your current network. Most people think of networking as reaching out to new people, but do not forget about the network that you already have. (Hint: You probably call them your friends and co-workers.) There is no need to wait to meet new people to start connecting others or sharing useful information. Network within the groups that are already close by.

Making networking a habit

Try to contact one person per day. If you reach out to five new people every week, that would be about 250 people per year.

Sending an email, text, or making a quick call will only take about five minutes of your day. Not everyone is going to get back to you, but if you contact that many new people, then you are bound to make significant progress.

Do not take "no" personally. Everyone is busy. For most people, it is simply a matter of timing. If you catch them on a good day, then they will happily talk or meet with you. If they are swamped, however, then a simple "no" might be all that you get. Do not take it to heart. In most cases, it is not a reflection of you or what you said.

Make it a point to follow up. One or two days after meeting someone for the first time, follow up with a brief email, text message, or note. This is an opportunity to develop the relationship by bringing up a topic that you discussed before or making a comment on an interesting topic. Following up with relevant conversation helps to anchor your previous interaction in their mind and displays more personality than just sending a message that says, "Thanks for talking!"

Did you fail? Try reaching out in a different way. You do not want to pester anyone, but if you give them a few weeks and do not hear a response, then there is nothing wrong with being persistent. For example, dropping in to talk face-to-face has resulted in great conversations with people that previously ignored my emails or text messages. Sometimes switching it up is all you need to do.

Things to remember

Network with the intention of helping other people, not yourself. People enjoy doing business with those that they trust and like. The only way to build that trust is to engage with others in a helpful way. Yes, trust takes a long time to build, but insincerity takes even longer to overcome. Once you have developed a relationship and created a bond, then you can move on to negotiating for favors and asking for help.

Networking is more about listening to what people say than saying the right things. Take the time to listen to people's stories. You can only provide something of value to them if you listen to who they are and what they do.

Sometimes the best networking opportunities involve real work. Volunteer for events, committees, projects that will have interesting people at them, or, even better, working for them. Working on a project or task with someone is one of the best ways to develop a relationship. For example, volunteering for a non-profit can be a great way to get to know their influential board members. I currently sit on two Boards of non-profits, am a regular at another and am a member in Rotary International. All started by increasing my Networking activities with the added benefit of giving back.

Email is easy to send…and ignore. Yes, email is quick, simple, and can be sent to anyone, anywhere. It is also very easy to be filtered out and ignored. If you really want to meet someone, then do not be afraid to pick up the phone, send a quick text message—preferable to email these days—or arrange a face-to-face meeting. These communication channels are usually less crowded and more personal, which means that your message will be more memorable. Email can be a great tool, but do not be afraid to mix it up.

What You Should Do Now

You do not need to be a master to start building your network. Just taking a moment to reach out is a big step that will help most people. Sharing useful information and connecting like-minded people are simple actions that everyone will appreciate.

Networking can make a huge difference if you focus on being useful and do not make things harder than they have to be.

You see, I have experienced some crazy stuff in my quest for true residual income. The first 25 years of my working life was purely transactional, and extremely educational. The next four years, 2000–2003, were transactional, trying to get to residual, mixed with bad investing of time and money, going broke; it was extremely educational, too. From 2004 until today, and for the rest of my life, it is completely, truly residual, magical, and it fits the new Connection Economy. But as you can see, it did not just happen. I would not wish some of these experiences on anyone, especially you reading this book. Get educated early on; the old saying of ignorance being bliss is dead wrong, ignorance will cost you, a lot.

Chapter 12

The Success Triangle

*"You can have everything in life you want
if you will just help enough other people get what they want."*

– Zig Ziglar

One of my early mentors in the quest for residual income was a young man in Texas by the name of Jerry Clark, who wrote the foreword for this book. Mr. Clark has an incredible story himself; he made millions, lost it all, then worked to get it all back again. The last time I spoke to Mr. Clark, he was telling me that he earns around $5,000 or more a day now—not bad for someone who dropped out of college! But it is not about the money for Mr. Clark, it is now about his personal mission: to help as many people as humanly possible to create their own incredible lifestyle, one which Mr. Clark knows is possible for anyone, anywhere. I am always impressed by his constant drive for knowledge: he is currently working on his master's degree and is one of the best read people I have ever known.

It was Mr. Clark's Success Triangle that made me truly understand my role in the creation of anything that I personally wanted out of life. It was a lesson I have visited many, many times, and one that I spend time training others on today. One of the greatest things we can leave others is the virtue of knowledge. Mr. Clark's Success Triangle left such an impression on me that I have passed it to hundreds of others. How many total people like myself do you think have done the same? That is the impact one person can have in a life, and I have been thankful to Mr. Clark for many years because of it.

So what is the Success Triangle? Well, here it is:

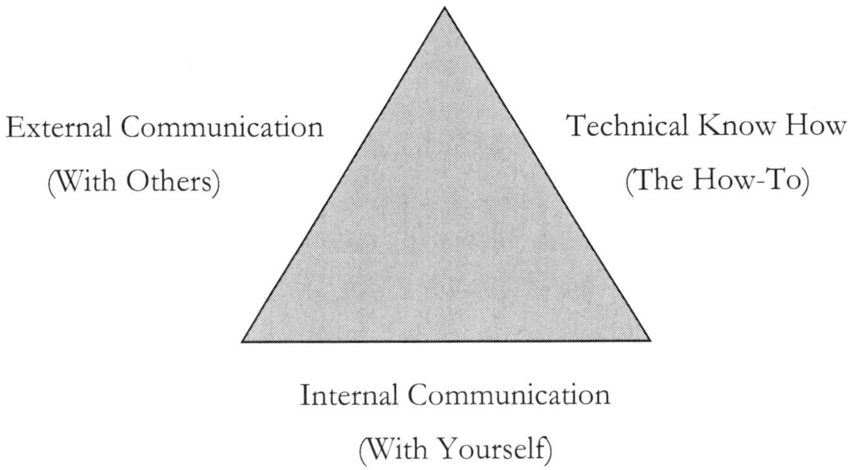

As you can see, the foundation of this triangle is the Internal Communication, how and what you say, think, and do inside you own mind! It goes directly back to what we spoke about in Chapters 2, 3, and 4. Success, or lack of success, in life and business has everything to do with your own personal philosophies, meaning, your beliefs, your mindset, and your convictions. Business Coach Jim Rohn once said that it is your personal philosophies that will allow you to get on in life. If you think things are hard, if you blame others for your lack of, if you blame the government, or your significant others, then you just do not get it. Your total success, or lack of, is a direct reflection of you; no one else is responsible. You are, period, end of story. Put a wrap on it!

Mr. Rohn was another one of my most valuable mentors as I was transitioning from being an employee to an entrepreneur; he has so many great quotes but one of my favorite is simple and to the point: "Don't wish it was easier, wish you were better."

You get better through the understanding that everything that happens in your life is a direct result of your beliefs. In my life, every time I had passion, belief, positive thoughts all the time, I was rocking and rolling and every time I became stuck in the mud with stinkin' thinkin', so were my results. It just is not rocket science ladies and gentlemen but throughout this book we have drilled it over and over again because it is, as Earl Nightingale, so elegantly stated in 1956, the strangest secret in the world!

One of the other very important principles upon which we need to touch here was first discussed in detail by Mr. Rohn, then put into a book called *The Slight Edge* by Jeff Olsen. Putting the principle into practice will pretty much guarantee your success in everything in your life. It will allow you to live a healthier life, will allow you to reach all your goals in life. Ralph Waldo Emerson, in his essay, "compensation," in 1841 spoke about this phenomenon. Mr. Emerson states it this way: "The law of nature is, do the thing, and you shall have the power; but they who do not the thing have not the power." I have been amazed over the years to watch literally thousands of people, all with the same opportunities, all living in the most prosperous country in the world, not "do the thing" and have no power. The "thing" is the ability to practice simple disciplines over time, or simple errors in judgment over that same time. It is the practice of simple discipline that will allow you to have whatever it is you want from life. On the other hand, it will be the simple errors in judgment, practiced over time, which will crater that which you had dreamt about.

Look at a couple of different examples here. If you knew that eating a lot of processed fast food was not good for your health, but you decide tomorrow to have one of those fast food hamburgers, would your health deteriorate? No, not usually. But it is that error in judgment, practiced over time that will get you in trouble with your overall health. Just look at our society today: those simple errors in judgment are literally killing us. I am sure that you have heard the old saying that "eating an apple a day will keep the doctor away"; well, as Jim Rohn astutely asked us, what if that was true? What if eating an apple a day would keep the doctor away? Why would not everyone do it?

It is because it is easy to do, certainly, but it is also easy not to do. Basically, everything that we need to do to be successful in our business is easy to do—there is very little to it, really—but it is also easy not to do, and that is where we get into trouble. If your business is reliant on building a database of ongoing customers, and to secure those customers you need to get out of your comfort zone, do some real networking, then why not just do it? Because it is easy to do, and easy not to do. That is why I have seen hundreds, maybe even thousands now, start something, and never finish it. But I have also seen a few follow the Slight Edge philosophy and totally change their lives. A very important principle in your personal philosophy, simple disciplines, such as networking or marketing, practiced over time or simple errors in judgment—"oh, I will do double work tomorrow"—practiced over that same time. It is a decision. And will make all the difference between success and failure.

Get good at this one thing, change your beliefs, your personal philosophies, get on top of your mind, get and stay positive, and you will be amazed at what your life will become!

On the left hand side of this triangle is External Communication, how to relate to others. This is also really important since in every discussion with anyone concerning whatever it is you are trying to get someone else to do, there is either tension or cooperation. Our goal is to always get to cooperation, especially in a business discussion. So getting good at your language, getting good at reading who it is you are speaking with, getting good at building relationships and getting good at pre talk, that is, finding an emotional anchor for whatever solution you may have in someone's life, is vitally important to be successful.

We could spend another whole book with just this discussion about External Communication, but to keep it simple, we will just discuss the way to go from tension to cooperation in any discussion with someone else.

You must understand the type of personality they have, and then relate right with them. In other words, you must be like a chameleon.

There are just four basic personality types that we have. There are dozens of books on these types and lots of tests given every year to assess personality types; many companies use personality profiles to analyze their workforce or potential new hires. Some call them four different colors, some different animal types, some stones and gems. For our exercise here, we are just going to talk about what these four styles are like. And you should get to know who you are, and a bit about each of the different styles in order to understand how to relate to others.

Everyone falls into one of these four styles:

1. *Those who are open and indirect.* These are the folks who always want to be part of a team, always want to get along, good team players, do not like conflict, they are all about relationships and communication, they want to be accepted and do not particularly like change. These are the patient ones with a peaceful demeanor, and seem to just go with the flow. They are 35 percent of the population and, as far as job

types go, would be the teachers, social workers, nurses, and so on.

2. *Those who are self-contained and indirect.* These folks are task-oriented, have a slow pace, are very analytical and can sometimes have paralysis through over-analysis. They have great follow-through skills, but are slow to make decisions since they want the decision to be right and not a reflection upon them if it is a bad decision. They are the problem-solvers and are persistent. They are also 35 percent of the population and are the accountants, engineers, and lawyers.
3. *Those who are self-contained and direct.* They are usually fast and decisive: all about the tasks and facts. These are the folks that we call natural-born leaders since they seem to take action towards goals regularly. They are the risk-takers, and we sometimes call these folks "Type-A" personalities or "drivers." They are 15 percent of the population and are the CEO's, military leaders, and entrepreneurs.
4. *Those who are open and direct.* They are all about relationships and interacting, really fast and spontaneous. They are usually the fun ones, want to be at every party, and even like to be the life of the party. Generally very good at promotion, they are not very good at follow-up. It is always about the money. They are 15 percent of the population and are the salesmen, the actors, entertainer, and, obviously the standup comic.

So, which one are you? Do you know? Everyone is one these types predominantly but everyone, depending upon circumstances, can have some of the other traits, too.

The goal with getting to cooperation from tension is to first identify who you are, and then be able to relate to the person you are having the discussion with. If you are trying to convince a prospect that they should be a client or buy from you, or join your sales team, etc., the better you get at identifying their personality behaviors, and the better you get mirroring that behavior, the better results you will have.

Here is a story that happened to me a few years ago that illustrates exactly how understanding the traits and then mirroring them works. One of my partners in California called me one day and asked if I would meet with a prospect for him; I agreed to do it. In the discussion about his prospect, he told me that he was working as a sales rep at one of the local wireless phone providers and that he had been there for 10 or 12 years. As I was preparing for this meeting, I initially determined that Mr. Prospect must be one of those open and direct individuals, being that he is in sales, and working in a wireless store. So I was prepared to tell him all about the team we have, the fun we have with our monthly parties, the income potential and the freedom that our business provides us and so on. I was ready.

As I sat down with this individual and we began some small talk, just getting acquainted, I asked him about his current job. It was then that he told me that he had been recently transferred into a store doing sales, which he really did not like all that much, but due to cutbacks in the headquarters, that was his only option. I then found out that this gent was in the accounting department of the company, and he loved to work the numbers each week. His job used to be to prepare a report for all the store managers each week detailing their sales, profits, and so on: he was a numbers guy! That changed my whole approach. I went from being prepared to talk to him like he was one of those open and direct types of individuals to someone that is self-contained and indirect. Instead of talking about the money, the team, the fun, I first took out my book of business, an impressive display of customers, facts, sales, which immediately took Mr. Prospect from one of a bit of tension—I mean, he did not know me from Adam—to one of cooperation, in which he started to immediately ask me questions and felt comfortable with me; he eventually joined our team.

The whole difference in approach here was to understand what makes Mr. Prospect tick. Stephen Covey, in one of the *7 Habits of Highly Effective People*, says it best: "Seek first to understand, then to be understood." If you understand who it is you are meeting with, attempting to sell too, or attempting to impress, then first talk to them like they want to be talked to. Be a chameleon.

The Technical Know-How

Okay, so now you have got your head straight, and you understand that it is all about Networking, which is all about getting folks to not only like you but also about relating to them—to go from a place of tension to cooperation, especially in a business setting.

The technical know-how is actually almost always the easiest, so relax. In fact, if you master the first one, internal communication, and then the second, external communication, then you are more than 90 percent of the way to success. The technical know-how is really what is in the book. It is the learning about the how-to and frankly, anyone can learn the how-to to virtually anything if they just put forth the effort to do so. If we are talking about a franchise, for example, then the technical know-how will be handed to you in a manual. If you have decided upon a business you can work from home, if you have done your homework really well and applied some of the principles in this book, then they—the company you selected to partner with as an Independent Contractor—will also have a manual, a website, and training for you to learn their system, their way of doing, and being.

The technical know-how is really a no brainer, and anyone can do it, anywhere, at any time. Really, what always gets in the way of building the successful business you may be looking for is the first two items, and 75 percent of it is really the internal communication.

That gent I spoke about earlier, Mr. Jerry Clark, tells a story about when he really started putting it all together with the success triangle. He was representing a Network Marketing company, one many of us have probably heard of and is very successful today, A.L. Williams, now called Primerica. This is the company that virtually changed the insurance industry. As a sales rep with A.L. Williams you had to learn quite a bit about the industry, the different types of insurance, and, in many States, had to be licensed; this is all technical know-how stuff.

Mr. Clark would have a three-hour training on Saturday morning and the new and existing sales team would show up to get trained on all these technical know-how topics. He would then release the troops to go make things happen. What Mr. Clark noticed the next week, and following weeks, was the fact that the same people would show up every Saturday morning. So, he and his partners decided that they must not be giving enough information so they increased the session to go from 8–12pm every Saturday. The same result would happen, so they changed it to 8–5pm every Saturday; the exact same thing would happen. The same folks for show up week after week and then go out for the week and nothing would happen, then they would show up again.

Well, Mr. Clark and his partners decided that maybe they just were not training these folks enough and so they started full Saturday and Sunday trainings, going over every single detail you would ever need to know about the insurance business and how it relates to A.L. Williams; everything about how to set up a new policy; what to say and how to say it; and how to Network and find new potential prospects. You get the idea. And guess what happened? Nothing. The same people would show up to get the technical know-how again. So it dawned on Mr. Clark that getting these folks to perform really had nothing to do with the technical know-how, they had all the information they would ever need. What he discovered was it was all about belief, all about convictions, mindset; all about having the confidence to simply do the job. It was all the stuff in the head, all the personal stuff we talk to ourselves about—and talk ourselves out of—that was the difference maker. And the Success Triangle was born.

So do not get too hyped-up on knowing everything about the company or business you select. Yes, make sure you understand the policies, the procedures, and the way of the company, but first really get clear that you are ready, you are confident, you have clarity of outcome, you know what you want, and how you will get there. You become what you think about. Think about all the right stuff.

Chapter 13

And Do Not Forget About

"Our new Constitution is now established, and has an appearance that promises permanency; but in this world nothing can be said to be certain, except death and taxes."

– Benjamin Franklin

Regardless of what type of business you decide upon, it will be important to get all the facts about various taxes, insurances, and other liabilities, both local, state or province, and federal. There is, unfortunately, a lot to get straight here, and it is certainly not for the lay person. My advice is to have a good lawyer, accountant, and bookkeeper that can handle all the requirements with a new or existing business.

And there all kinds of online resources that will help you maneuver through the organizational maze and legalese necessary for your particular area and selected industry or business. Some of those resources include www.sba.gov, www.legalzoom.com, www.dsa.org, and www.franchisedirect.com.

If your decision is one that allows you to work from home, that is an even more important process to ensure that even though you may have an office at home, you treat your business like a business and you have separation of home-life and work-life. If this is new to you, you might find the transition to be a bit difficult at first, unless you have some strong organizational and discipline skills to help you along the way. I believe that I have those skills, and I found my transition from a corporate environment to a small office outside the home to a work-from-home environment to be quite a transition. Today there are many locations which offer independent work environments, incubators, and so on that you may even want to consider.

I have taught certain rules, seven to be exact, for those transitioning to a business from home. Operating your business from your house combines your work and the rest of your life. With both of these life aspects located in one space, you will need to develop a new set of disciplines. Here are seven factors that you need to consider in setting up your home office.

Priorities from each aspect of your life will be competing for your attention. There will be days when you feel that answering emails needs to be tackled first before laundry. But there will be days when you will feel that your first important job for the day will be your laundry (that is usually Monday mornings for me!).

To help you ensure productivity, consider the following specifics when you are setting up your home office and choosing a site for your home office in your house.

1. Establish your home office in a part of the house that has lots of light and air. Think about the year-round conditions in this spot, not just what it is like during the season in which you are setting up your home office. In buying lighting, match the type to task. Ambient lighting, which lights up the room, should be uniform and moderately bright. You may also want to have overhead lighting and floor lamps. Also keep the room from getting stuffy by providing the proper ventilation to the room. Choose a space with windows that you can open to keep air circulating.
2. Set-up shop away from the busy areas in your home. Make sure your home office is as far as possible from potential distractions such as the kitchen, front door, family traffic, and a lot of noise. This is especially important if you have children and will have child care in the house during the day. If you can see or hear your children and they can see you, it will be difficult for both you and your children.
3. Organize your supplies. Similar to a corporate environment, you need to arrange your supplies in a way that promotes efficiency. You need not lift two stacks of paper just to get to your business stationery located at the furthermost end of your cabinet. Hide supplies that you do not need every day such as extra rolls of tape and piles of paper but keep within

reach a small cache of supplies at your desk or near enough that you can reach them. Stack extra supplies under your desk, out of kicking range. If space permits, keep extra supplies in a cabinet or cupboard.

4. Set up things so they function smoothly. Maximize the layout of your home office space with the goal of promoting efficiency of operations foremost in the design. Arrange your things to help you function better. For example, my landline (almost obsolete), fax machine (ditto) and cell phone are always on my left, my copiers on my right, all within arm's length, with my computer and keyboard comfortable right in front of me.
5. Limit the things in your home office to items that you need for your business. Clear out all of the old clutter in your home office area. If you set-up your home office in your attic, make sure that you have enough room for all your requirements. It is difficult to work in a place filled with items irrelevant to your business. However, if you cannot remove these things from the room, make sure that you move them out of your vision. Creating visual and psychological separation by enclosing the area with a screen or a decorative barrier could be a way to address this problem. Tidiness of the office environment can help improve your productivity.
6. A home office does not need to be a separate room. If space is an issue, you can simply set-up a table and a chair in one corner of a room. You can also use the space underneath the stairways, the space at the end of hallways, or the loft space and landing between floors. Some even work in a nook off the kitchen. The important thing is that you can have a permanent workspace that is dedicated to your work. The disadvantage of this set-up, though, is the potential for distraction.
7. Have a dedicated work area. The ideal situation is to have a permanent room for your work area, both from a productivity and taxation point of view. A distinct workspace helps condition your mind that this is a place where you do work. Moreover, having a separate area that is used exclusively and regularly for your business is an important

criterion to qualify for tax deductions for your home office. If you are prepared to do some renovations, you can consider converting your attic, basement, deck off the living room or kitchen, carport, or garage into your very own home office.

About Taxes and Tax Deductions:

One of the privileges of having a home-based business is the tax advantages that the U.S. and Canadian governments have for those operating a home-based businesses. The U.S. government wants American workers to be independent and self-employed, thus the tax code is favorable for home-based businesses.

Three things to know about your home-based business:

1. If you are operating as an Independent Contractor, the company you are representing will send you what is called a Form 1099 at year's end if you have earned $600 or more for the calendar year. This form documents the amount of commissions and bonuses you have earned for the year. If you are a sole proprietor, make sure to have a program, such as Quick Books, to list your revenues and expenses monthly.

   Note that the income you earn throughout the year is taxable income and, depending upon your tax bracket, should be put aside and/or filed quarterly with the IRS. Consult a tax adviser for details.
2. The amount that you will be able to deduct from your income earned is totally dependent upon a good record keeper. If you keep your receipts for *everything* you do with the business and use a monthly tracking system to capture all your revenues, expenses and other costs and considerations; this will make it very easy for a tax adviser at year-end.
3. Use a tax accounting spreadsheet to track everything monthly so as not to miss any of the benefits to having a home-based business.

As the IRS requires written documentation to qualify for the deduction, *now* is the time to start keeping your receipts! Make it a habit right from the beginning.

If you are operating as a home-based business, here is a list of potential deductions for your business; again, consult your professional lawyers, accountants, and bookkeepers for all the insights for your particular situation.

<u>Your Home Office</u>: As mentioned, create one area in your house to do your business from. It can be out of a closet, a desk in the corner of a room, a full room, or an office created out of some of your garage space, the only requirement is that it be used exclusively for business. The percentage of the house used for business calculates the part of the following that you can deduct from your taxes (document with receipts):

- Rent (If you own your home with the bank, the interest, taxes, etc. are applied elsewhere)
- Electrical bill
- Sewer bill
- Insurance (not deductible at all, unless you have a home business!)
- Cleaning service (as long as they clean where your office is too!)
- Garbage service
- Water bill
- House repairs
- Landscaping (if people come to your house on business)

<u>Personal Training Expenses</u> (Document with receipts)

- Seminars attended
- Books
- CD / DVD programs
- Training conference calls

<u>Advertising Expenses</u>: Any logo gear can be seen by the public, and is thus an advertising expense.

- Giving it as a gift? Treat as advertising
- Newspaper ads
- County fair/expo booth fees
- Fliers

- Product Samples
- Company literature
- Reproduction costs (photocopies, etc.)

Labor Expenses paid to your children for business related work: Keep track of what is done, and how much paid, pay by check, canceled check is proof. No Social Security or income taxes need to be paid on your children!

- Emptying the garbage
- Mowing lawn and other landscaping
- Cleaning your office
- Filing
- Computer work
- Envelope stuffing/postcard stamping and other mailing tasks
- Other business related items

Business Travel

- Convention
- Travel to pre-arranged presentations
- Airfare, train fare, and car mileage
- All "fees" related to travel/parking, tolls, security, etc.
- Meals while on the trip (subject to limitations, usually 50 percent deductible)
- Entertainment expenses (subject to some rules and limitations)
- Out of area training

Office Expenses

- Paper clips
- Printer paper and toner
- Light bulbs
- Pens, pencils, and highlighters
- Whiteboards
- Easels and presentation flip charts

- Furnishings (chairs, desks, lamps, carpet, etc.)
- Equipment (computers, printers, fax machines, phones, etc.)
- Phone bill (if you only have one phone, only the long distance calls related to business, the IRS believes that one line is a necessity and will not allow that as a deduction)
- Special services on your phone bill (three-way calling, call waiting, voice mail)
- Second line used for business (document business usage by adding to your business card/stationery)
- Cell Phone (document business usage by adding to your business card/stationery)
- E-mail (document business usage by adding to your business card/stationery)
- Postage for business mailings

Business Meals When you do a presentation at a restaurant/coffee shop, pick up your receipt! This is a deductible expense (50 percent).

Celebration Expenses Giving a party to celebrate success? Invite your business associates/prospects and deduct the entire cost. Document via receipts and invitation list, have attendees sign a "guest book" to document who attended.

In-home expenses

- Baby Sitters
- Product cases (for carrying display product in/out of house)
- Demonstration supplies
- Assistants
- Food provided (100 percent)
- Snacks/Tea/Coffee/Shakes (100 percent)

Mileage to/from presentations, training events, etc. Document with mileage log. Do for three consecutive months, or three like periods, extrapolate totals to full year (multiply by four). IRS requires some sort of logical, written documentation of this. If your day planner does not have a good sheet for this, check out the web for one, or make your own. It needs date, purpose, start mileage, end mileage, total mileage on the trip, and total mileage for the month. You will also need the year's start and ending mileage numbers off of your car's odometer for the tax form.

Taxes are a *very* complex issue, and no widespread communication like this would be complete without the boilerplate disclaimer:

All of the above information is advisory and educational. It MAY NOT apply to you and your circumstances in any given year. In addition, tax laws of the land change quite frequently, as your tax professional will tell you. If you have any questions about your specific situation, consult a qualified tax professional.

Finally, you know your personal situation better than anyone will from a 45-minute interview at tax time. I would highly suggest that you purchase a copy of tax software or its equivalent and prepare your own taxes for submission or for organizing yourself before visiting your tax professional for the final "tweaks" and areas the program does not cover. It will save you *a lot* of money either way, and is tax deductible to boot.

If you have your taxes completed each year by a professional, the time spent organizing your paperwork for a computer tax program will reduce your fees, because the accountant will save time by not having to organize them for you; raise your knowledge level so you can give your accountant all they need to qualify you for all the deductions you deserve; allow you to better evaluate your accountant's services, as they relate to your situation; and improve your filing system to reduce your time and fees even more for next year.

Chapter 14

Okay...So What Now?

"When there is no hope in the future there is no power in the present."

– John Maxwell

We have just been through a whole lot of information in this book, and if you are somewhat confused, you should not be. What that usually means is that you are still looking at "what now" with your head, not your heart. Think with your heart; what does your heart tell you after getting this information? Finding your purpose, your passion, and then making sure you are doing it to be able to leave a legacy and have the money and time freedom to live that life on purpose is what you are all about. It is what should drive you every day. If you do not have that, and you have read this far, then you are still searching. You know that you do not want to be someone else's employee the rest of your life, but the fear of making a move, the fear of just doing something different is holding you back.

Remember what we said about fear: false expectations appearing real. It appears real, but it is not real. If you have a strong enough why, if you allow your why and you heart to meet up, then you will find the perfect business for you, and the correct time for you. You will have enough education, the brainpower by having this book, that it will assist you every step of the way. You will be able to look at any type of business and be able to identify it has a legitimate, authentic type business with a product or service trending positively (a swan) or an inauthentic company, product or service (a duck) which will just cost you time, money, and misery.

You can now easily differentiate the difference between transactional income and residual income. You now understand why the different Quadrants—E, S, B and I—are so different when it comes to transactional versus residual. You now understand leverage and how it is leverage that creates true residual income.

You now know that not only are your philosophies, your beliefs, and your self-talk going to put you in the driver's seat or the outhouse, but you also know how important it is to be a chameleon. How our words, our language, what we say to others, and how we say it will either breed contempt—flight—or cooperation. Never underestimate the power of the words you speak. And you now know that anyone can learn the technical details of any such business endeavor; that is the easy part!

So it is up to you. It is now your turn to have the life you are meant to have, the time for you and your significant others; it is the life that most people will never have because they will not pick up this book, or take any action to achieve what they really want out of life.

I would like to end with a poem, one that was shared with me years ago, and has shown up in my life more than once. It has meaning and, as with every great poem, should be read between the lines. The poem "If" by Rudyard Kipling:

> If you can keep your head when all about you
> Are losing theirs and blaming it on you,
> If you can trust yourself when all men doubt you,
> But make allowance for their doubting too;
> If you can wait and not be tired by waiting,
> Or being lied about, do not deal in lies,
> Or being hated, do not give way to hating,
> And yet do not look too good, nor talk too wise:
>
> If you can dream—and not make dreams your master;
> If you can think—and not make thoughts your aim;
> If you can meet with Triumph and Disaster
> And treat those two impostors just the same;
> If you can bear to hear the truth you have spoken
> Twisted by knaves to make a trap for fools,
> Or watch the things you gave your life to, broken,
> And stoop and build 'em up with worn-out tools:
>
> If you can make one heap of all your winnings

And risk it on one turn of pitch-and-toss,
And lose, and start again at your beginnings
And never breathe a word about your loss;
If you can force your heart and nerve and sinew
To serve your turn long after they are gone,
And so hold on when there is nothing in you
Except the Will which says to them: 'Hold on!'

If you can talk with crowds and keep your virtue,
Or walk with Kings—nor lose the common touch,
If neither foes nor loving friends can hurt you,
If all men count with you, but none too much;
If you can fill the unforgiving minute
With sixty seconds' worth of distance run,
Yours is the Earth and everything that is in it,
And—which is more—you will be a Man, my son!

I am truly grateful to share many thoughts, insights, triumphs, and disasters with you and I thank you for allowing me to share in hopes that the rest of your life on this earth is filled with passion, purpose, love, and giving something back. Pass it on; pass this book on to someone you might know that could glean the same insights you now have. Be well, my friend.

Extras

APPENDIX

Preface

Page xi – "Deloitte's Shift Index Survey," www.businessinsider.com

Page xi – www.happyplanetindex.com

Page xii – *Start With Why: How Great Leaders Inspire Everyone to Take Action*, Simon Sinek, www.startwithwhy.com, The Penguin Group, 2009

Page xii – CBS News, June 20, 2013, cbsnews.com

Introduction

Page 1 – "The New Normal," McKinsey and Company, March 2009

Page 1 – U.S. Bureau of Labor Statistics, www.bls.gov

Page 3 – *The Purple Cow, The Tribe, Linchpin, The Icarus Deception*, Seth Godin, The Penguin Group, 2012

Page 4 – "Survey of American savings," www.bankrate.com, 2013

Chapter 1: Experiences of a Lifetime

Page 9 – *The Icarus Deception*, Seth Godin, The Penguin Group, 2012

Page 10 – *The Cash Flow Quadrant, Rich Dad's Guide to Financial Freedom*, Robert T Kiyosaki with Sharon L Lechter, CPA, Business Plus, Hachette Book Group, May 2000

Page 11 – *Why A Students Work for C Students, and B Students work for the Government*, Robert T Kiyosaki, Plata Publishing, April 9, 2013

Chapter 2: The New Normal—The Connection Economy

Page 16 – *The Icarus Deception*, Seth Godin, The Penguin Group, 2012

Page 18 – www.doallrshaveclub.com; Dollar Shave Club, Mark Levine and Michael Dublin, 2011

Page 19 – The Duce, www.theducephx.com

Page 19 – Scott Dinsmore, www.liveyourlegend.net

Page 19 – *The E-Myth Revisited*, Michael Gerber, HarperCollins; 2nd Edition, 2003

Page 21 – Seth Godin Blog Entry, www.sethgodin.com, June 20, 2013

Chapter 3: Do You Know "Why"?

Page 24, 28 – *Start With Why: How Great Leaders Inspire Everyone to Take Action*, Simon Sinek, www.startwithwhy.com, The Penguin Group, 2009

Page 25 – Scott Dinsmore, www.liveyourlegend.net

Page Jim Rohn International, www.jimrohn.com

Chapter 4: Start with Belief

Page 35 – *The Biology of Belief: Unleashing the Power of Consciousness*, Bruce Lipton, Matter, and Miracles (2005–8 Hay House U. S. Publisher)

Page 35 – Ap Dijkersterhuis and Loran Nordgren of the University of Amsterdam, http://www.uva.nl/en/home

Page 37 – *Linchpin: Are You Indispensable?* Seth Godin The Penguin Group, 2011

Page 38 – *The Strangest Secret in the World*, Earl Nightingale, 1956

Page 39 – Franklin Covey, Inc. www.franklincovey.com; Free Mission Statement Tool, www.franklincovey.com/msb/

Chapter 5: Mining Your Passion

Page 42 – "Passion," www.wikipedia.com

Page 46 – Jerry Clark, www.clubrhino.net , Dallas, Texas

Page 47 – "Passion Workbook," Scott Dinsmore, www.liveyourlegend.com

Chapter 6: Perfect Business, Inc.

Page 50 – Dr. Ken Dychtwald, Age Wave, Inc., www.agewave.com

Page 51 – Jason Dorsey, Center for Generational Kinetics, www.genhq.com

Page 53 – "Diffusion of Innovation," www.wikipedia.org

Page 53 – *Start With Why: How Great Leaders Inspire Everyone to Take Action*, Simon Sinek, www.startwithwhy.com, The Penguin Group, 2009

Page 53 – Jim Rohn International, www.jimrohn.com

Chapter 7: Transactional vs. Residual

Page 56 – *The Cash Flow Quadrant, Rich Dad's Guide to Financial Freedom*, Robert T Kiyosaki with Sharon L Lechter, CPA, Business Plus, Hachette Book Group, May 2000

Page 57 – United States Small Business Administration, SBA, www.sba.gov

Page 61 – "The Terrible Towel and Myron Cope," www.wikipedia.org

Chapter 8: So You Have a Business Idea?

Page 63 – "The Fortune 500 Listing," www.money.cnn.com/fortune500

Page 67 – "Business Models," www.wikipedia.org

Chapter 9: It Must be 'Truly'

Page 74 – *The Cash Flow Quadrant, Rich Dad's Guide to Financial Freedom*, Robert T Kiyosaki with Sharon L Lechter, CPA, Business Plus, Hachette Book Group, May 2000

Page 75 – *It Must Be Truly* Co-Written by Mark Atha, Scottsdale AZ and Rick Jongkind, Vancouver, BC, Canada and Harvey Hess, Chandler AZ

Chapter 10: Deeper Dive

Page 85 – *Linchpin: Are You Indispensable?* Seth Godin The Penguin Group, 2011

Page 85 – *The Icarus Deception*, Seth Godin, The Penguin Group, 2012

Page 85 – Self-Employment: www.about.com; Small Business: Canada

Page 88 – "Independent Contractor," www.wikipedia.org

Page 92 – McDonalds Franchise Opportunity, www.aboutmcdonalds.com/mcd/franchising

Page 96 – "MLM," www.wikipedia.org

About 99 – Network Marketing, www.about.com

Chapter 11: Is It A Duck?

Page 102 – *Escape From Cubicle Nation: From Corporate Prisoner to Thriving Entrepreneur*, Pamela Slim, The Berkeley Publishing Group, 2009

Page 116 – *People of the State of California v James A Sweeney II and Patrick M Ryan*, The Big Co-op

Page 118 – Word-of-Mouth Marketing Organization, www.womma.org

Page 118 – Becoming a BzzAgent, www.bzzagent.com

Page 119 – Direct Selling Association, www.dsa.org

Chapter 12: The Success Triangle

Page 127 – Jerry Clark, www.clubrhino.net, Dallas, Texas

Page 128 – Jim Rohn International, www.jimrohn.com

Page 129 – *The Slight Edge*, Jeff Olson, Success / Books, 2005

Page 133 – *The Seven Habits of Highly Effective People*, Stephen Covey, Simon and Schuster, 1990

Chapter 13: And Do Not Forget About...

Page 135 – The U.S. Small Business Administration, www.sba.gov

Page 135 – Legal Zoom Legal Documents, www.legalzoom.com

Page 135 – Franchising Directory, www.franchisedirect.com

Page 135 – Direct Selling Association, www.dsa.org

Page 138 – "All About U.S. Taxes," www.irs.gov

Page 138 – "All About Canadian Taxes," www.taxes.ca

Page 138 – Tax Professionals, www.natptax.com

Chapter 14: Okay, So What Now?

Page 144 – "If" by British Nobel Laureate Rudyard Kipling

DEFINITION OF TERMS

Industrial Economy

Generally speaking, the industrial economy concerns those activities combining factors of production (facilities, supplies, work, knowledge) to produce material goods intended for the market. Sometimes called the Industrial Revolution, it was a period from the 18th to the 19th century where major changes in agriculture, manufacturing, mining, transport, and technology had a profound effect on the socioeconomic and cultural conditions starting in the United Kingdom, then subsequently spreading throughout Europe, North America, and eventually the world. The Industrial Revolution marks a major turning point in human history.

Baby Boomers

Baby Boomers are people born during the demographic Post–World War II baby boom between the years 1946 and 1964. As a group, they were the wealthiest, most active, and most physically fit generation up to that time, and amongst the first to grow up genuinely expecting the world to improve with time. They were also the generation that received peak levels of income, therefore they could reap the benefits of abundant levels of food, apparel, retirement programs, and sometimes even "midlife crisis" products. The increased consumerism for this generation has been regularly criticized as excessive.

Generation X

Generation X, commonly abbreviated to Gen X, is the generation born after the Western Post–World War II baby boom. Demographers, historians, and commentators use beginning birth dates from 1965 to 1980. Compared with previous generations, Generation X represents a more apparently heterogeneous generation, openly acknowledging and embracing social diversity in terms of such characteristics as race, class, religion, ethnicity, culture, language, gender identity, and sexual orientation. Unlike their parents who challenged leaders with an intent to replace them, Gen Xers are less likely to idolize leaders and are more inclined to work toward long-term institutional and systematic change through economic, media and consumer actions. The U.S. Census Bureau reports that Generation X statistically holds the highest education levels when looking at current age groups.

Generation Y

Generation Y(also known as the Millennial Generation or Gen Y) are the demographic cohort following Generation X. Researchers and commentators use birth years from 1980 to the early 2000s. Sometimes referred as "Trophy Kids", a term that reflects the trend in competitive sports, as well as many other aspects of life, where mere participation is frequently enough for a reward. It has been reported that this is an issue in corporate environments. Some employers are concerned that Gen Y's have too great expectations from the workplace. Studies predict that they will switch jobs frequently, holding many more jobs than Gen Xers due to their great expectations. Gen Y's have been described as optimistic, engaged, and team players.

New Normal

New Normal is a term in business and economics that refers to financial conditions following the financial crisis of 2007-2008 and the aftermath of the 2008–2012 global recession. The term has since been used in a variety of other contexts to imply that something which was previously abnormal has become commonplace. It has been described as a cliché.

Connection Economy

The ongoing reduction of the industrial economy and the new normal from the aftermath of the financial crisis has created a void, which is being filled by a new economy, the connection economy. The connection economy rewards value created by building relationships and fostering connections, rather than assets and "stuff," like the industrial economy. The industrial economy values more, better, faster, whereas the connection economy builds on who you know, what you know and how that knowledge influences your connections.

Entrepreneurship

The capacity and willingness to develop, organize and manage a business venture along with any of its risks in order to make a profit. The most obvious example of entrepreneurship is the starting of new businesses.

In economics, entrepreneurship combined with land, labor, natural resources and capital can produce profit. Entrepreneurial spirit is characterized by innovation and risk-taking, and is an essential part of a nation's ability to succeed in an ever changing and increasingly competitive global marketplace.

Business Model

The plan implemented by an individual or company to generate revenue and make a profit from operations. The model includes the components and functions of the business, as well as the revenues it generates and the expenses it incurs. The business model dates back to the earliest days of business; it merely describes the way in which a company makes money. A business model can be simple or very complex. A restaurant's business model is to make money by cooking and serving food to hungry customers. A website's business model might not be so clear, as there are many ways in which these types of businesses can generate revenue. For example, some make money by providing a free service and then selling advertising to other companies, while others might sell a product or service directly to online customers.

Disruptive Business Model

Disruptive business models focus on creating, disintermediating, refining, re-engineering or optimizing a product/service, role/function/practice, category, market, sector, or industry. The most successful companies incorporate disruptive thinking into all of their business and management practices to gain distinctive competitive value propositions. "Me Too" companies fight to eke out market share in an attempt to survive, while disruptive companies become category dominant brands insuring sustainability.

Transactional Income

Personal income derived from the one time sale of an item, or the time invested, either salary or hourly, in a job or function, work performed. The cleanest definition is time for money, the investment of an individual's time for the monetary compensation for that time, or one time sale.

Residual Income

Personal income derived from the sale of an item, or work performed, that continues over time. You can also receive residual income from the invention of something of value that is utilized by others, or by the writing, performing, acting that is purchased and / or viewed on an ongoing basis.

Law of Consumerism

The criteria a person who is purchasing an item, i.e. the consumer, evaluates in order to make that purchase. Although the criteria is basically the same, need, price, value, convenience, the factors are weighted differently for each individual, based upon current circumstances. An example would be someone who needs an item right now (like a new Air Conditioner in the desert during the summer), need and convenience would rate higher than price or value whereas someone living at or below the poverty level, price weighs highest, almost always.